Taking Back
Your Life

Taking Back Your Life

WOMEN and PROBLEM GAMBLING

Diane Rae Davis, Ph.D.

HAZELDEN®

Hazelden
Center City, Minnesota 55012
hazelden.org

Library of Congress Cataloging-in-Publication Data

Davis, Diane Rae.
   Taking back your life : women and problem gambling / Diane Rae Davis. — 1st ed.
      p.   cm.
   Includes bibliographical references.
   ISBN 978-1-59285-732-6 (softcover)
   1. Women.   2. Gambling.   I. Title.
   HQ1206.D343 2009
   616.85'8416—dc22

                                                                                    2009011503

Editor's note
The stories in this book are true. Names, locations, and other identifying information have been changed to protect confidentiality.

Permission granted to reprint Are You Living with a Compulsive Gambler? and Suggestions for the Newcomer, from the Gam-Anon Web site at www.gam-anon. org, copyrighted by Gam-Anon International Service Office, Inc., P.O. Box 157, Whitestone, NY 11357.

Permission granted to reprint the Gamblers Anonymous Twelve Steps to Recovery and Twenty Questions, from the Gamblers Anonymous Web site at www.gamblers anonymous.org, copyrighted by Gamblers Anonymous International Service Office, P.O. Box 17173, Los Angeles, CA 90017.

13 12 11 10 09 1 2 3 4 5 6

Cover and interior design by Theresa Jaeger Gedig
Typesetting by BookMobile Design & Publishing Services

Contents

▓ ▓ ▓

Acknowledgments

■ ■ ■

This book would not exist without the honesty and generosity of the women who participated in the 2000–2001 Internet survey known as the "Women who have taken their life back from compulsive gambling" project. By sharing their experience, strength, and hope, they are a lesson to us all, showing that change can occur in even the most dire circumstances.

Two key people at Hazelden Publishing brought the book to life: thanks to Sid Farrar, editorial and trade director, for reading an unsolicited manuscript and taking a chance on me, and to editor Catherine Broberg for really understanding the intent of this book and pruning and shaping to make it happen.

I also thank Eastern Washington University for granting me a sabbatical leave so that I could actually sit down and write without the distractions of an academic life. Finally, I thank my family in Texas for keeping me grounded, more or less, during that journey.

Foreword

■ ■ ■

I met Dr. Diane Davis in 2001 when she interviewed me about my gambling problem. She listened carefully while I shared my painful journey. Now she has authored *Taking Back Your Life: Women and Problem Gambling*, which I believe should be required reading for suffering gamblers and their families.

When we met, Diane had just launched a Web site to survey more than 250 women and how they reached a recovery stage, and she interviewed some of these women in person. Women shared their most intimate feelings, and Diane listened. Through the numerous interviews she conducted, she developed a typical timeline for female addiction to gambling, from the first coin dropped into a machine to the devastating "bottom"—the low point that the gambler eventually experiences. She describes the lengths the gambler will go to: hiding the problem, inventing lies, manipulating everyone around her. Diane also explains the various levels the gambler must work through to build a foundation for recovery. We learn through this book how we can take our lives back. Throughout these chapters, she notes the differences between male and female gamblers regarding guilt, emotions, and decisions. She uncovers the reasons gamblers escape into their addiction and why they feel it is a safe place.

My own recovery dates back more than seventeen years, and through the years I have read dozens of books on gambling, particularly on female gambling. Unfortunately there were not many books that helped. Most of them were written in technical language and focused on theories and statistics, not on real human experience. I needed a book that spoke to me, not one filled with psychobabble. I needed to stop the pain now! This book meets that need.

Diane's book taught me how my brain processes the various factors associated with addiction, particularly the pleasure high. I realize now why I kept returning to the casino after constantly losing. Diane covers the difficult parts of working through recovery, offering suggestions on how to overcome these complex issues.

She describes the diagnostic instruments used to identify pathological gambling, which in turn help the gambler face the truth and make decisions. Admitting to the problem is a huge step. Her description of the Twelve Step program Gamblers Anonymous leaves no question unanswered and includes helpful examples of "working the Steps." The opportunity to identify with other gamblers and realize the availability of hope and strength is beneficial in the beginning of recovery. It is the first time many women are able to share the truth about their gambling addiction. The interviews excerpted in this book chart the women's journeys from these difficult first steps to the most satisfying part of recovery.

This book will be a great tool for all women struggling with gambling problems, but it will be particularly helpful for those in small towns, hidden in the outskirts of large cities and too far from meetings, counselors, or other types of recovery support. It will also speak to women in countries where help is not readily available, answering their questions as well. We are all aware that gambling is here to stay, and the help needed for recovery will increase.

The personal stories and information in this book will also be beneficial for the loved ones of problem gamblers. Diane describes the benefits of the Gam-Anon program, a Twelve Step program designed to support the family and friends of gamblers (similar to the relationship of Al-Anon to Alcoholics Anonymous). Gam-Anon members are offered answers to questions that have baffled them for years. Becoming a member of this program is a valuable tool to building and maintaining a more spiritual life for the family.

This book also lists resources and Web sites where further support and answers may be found.

Taking Back Your Life is about recovery and hope, and how the female gambler can reclaim her life. I highly recommend it for the gambler, for the counselor, for students in the addiction field in colleges and universities, and for everyone who wishes to understand gambling addiction.

■ ■ ■ **Marilyn Lancelot**

Marilyn Lancelot is the author of *Gripped by Gambling* and cofounder of the "Women Helping Women" Web site, www .femalegamblers.info.

Introduction

■ ■ ■

In the year 2000, I discovered one of my dearest friends was addicted to gambling. Her addiction had started out so innocently: one day, Sherry took her elderly mother on an outing to see the brand-new casino on the outskirts of her rural hometown. Later, when her mother became chronically ill, the casino became a place where Sherry could occasionally escape from the stress of caretaking. Like some casinos, this one was dry: it served no alcohol. Sherry is a recovering alcoholic of many years, and she was absolutely delighted to find an alcohol-free venue where she could still "get away from it all."

During the many weekends when she commuted to her mother's home to help her, Sherry sometimes tucked her in at night and then headed out to the casino for a few hours of "not thinking about what was happening." The respite excuse morphed into pure escapism as her mother's condition deteriorated. Once Sherry sat down to the Wheel of Fortune game and started placing bets, she didn't have a thought about her mother or the problems ahead. The flashing lights, the buzzing of the crowd, and the occasional alignment of a small winning combination lulled her into a kind of trance. Once in a while she won more money than she lost, but winning was not really the point anymore. She had found a successful way to escape.

After her mother's death, the inheritance Sherry received provided a means to keep on gambling—and for higher stakes. Sherry discovered many more casinos beyond the one in her old hometown. In fact, within fifty miles of her own home she found five of them, one a major "destination resort."

Instead of facing the grief of her mother's death, Sherry just kept on gambling. "The inheritance didn't seem like real money anyway," she says. During the next few years, she periodically tried to limit the money and time she spent gambling and was amazed at the difficulty of that task. She tried various methods that made sense to her, but nothing worked. Leaving her credit cards at home only resulted in a forty-mile round trip to get them after she ran out of cash at the casino. When she told herself she would only spend two hours at the casino, she found that she didn't leave until hours later when her money had run out.

When Sherry finally told me what was going on, she had been gambling for five years. I was astounded. I thought I knew her so well. How had she managed to keep this hidden for so long? How was she able to continue to work full-time and lead what looked like a normal life? And what kind of friend was I? I hadn't even noticed. Sherry was still struggling, so my first thought was to read the research literature and find out what was working for other women. Much to my surprise, I found very little written about women with gambling problems, and even less on how they successfully stopped.

Sherry's experience opened my eyes to a compulsive behavior facing women in our country, a problem I had not imagined before. I wondered how women were recovering from this problem, or *if* they were recovering. These questions became more important to me as I learned about the many women in longtime recovery from alcohol and drugs who then succumb to a gambling addiction. I was well aware of the proliferation of casinos in our country, but I had naively assumed that it was mostly men who were gambling there. A walk through the several casinos in the area made it clear that women were gambling as never before. And when they found themselves in trouble, many of them—like my friend Sherry—had trouble finding anyone to guide or encourage them in the recovery process. The local Gamblers Anonymous groups at that time consisted primarily of men. In contrast to the local Alcoholics Anonymous groups, there was no core of women who had worked the Twelve Steps and were available for sponsorship. No gambling addiction treatment programs were available locally, or even within Washington state.

What started as mere questions about how to help and support my friend grew into a broader quest for answers on this important topic. I decided to try to find out for myself whether and how women were recovering from compulsive gambling. Since I am a university professor, I naturally turned to the tools of academia for my search. At that time, most of the articles on gambling research were based on male experience, and finding information about the unique experiences of women proved extremely difficult. I decided to use the Internet to find women who had successfully quit their problem gambling and were willing to share their stories about how they did it.

The Internet Survey

That July, with the help of my university's media and technical staff, I launched a Web site designed to recruit women to respond to a survey and share their experience about how they recovered from gambling problems. ("Recovery" is a term used in Twelve Step programs to indicate people who are not only abstinent from an addictive behavior, but are also working on becoming a better person, mentally, spiritually, and emotionally.) In the survey, I asked participants to respond only if they had six months or more of abstinence from compulsive gambling. The Web site stated the purpose of the study and described how to participate in a 79-item survey (reprinted in the appendix) and/or a personal interview. It assured responders of their anonymity: their email addresses would be blocked from my view. It also included a project approval statement from the Human Subjects Review Board and links to various problem gambling sites that might be helpful to the respondents.

Of all the challenges involved with formulating this project, one of the most delicate was finding four women on campus at my university who would agree to have their pictures posted on the home page of a Web site on compulsive gambling. We finally solved the problem by screening their faces so they could not be recognized.

Publicizing the Web site so women in recovery could find it was another challenge. It took several months to be picked up by the major Internet search engines such as Google. Eventually, we had direct links from the National Council on Problem Gambling site, various state agency sites, and several other sites that help problem gamblers, such as "Women Helping Women" at www.female gamblers.info.

The survey site was fully functional and online from the latter part of 2000 through 2001. During that time, 264 women from all over the United States with varying lengths of abstinence completed the survey; 136 of them had not gambled at all for six months or more (for an average of about three years). These were the consistently abstinent women I had been seeking, and this book focuses on their data and their stories.

Fifteen of the 136 were recruited for personal in-depth interviews. These women were extremely generous with their time and willingness to tell me the details of their harrowing journey through compulsive gambling to recovery. Excerpts from these interviews appear throughout this book to illustrate these women's experiences. Great care has been taken to keep the interviewees anonymous by giving them different names and removing any identifying information.

The goal of the Internet survey was to give voice to these women's experience in three general areas:

1. How did gambling become a problem for you?
2. How did you stop gambling?
3. How were social supports (family members, friends, professional help, self-help) helpful or not helpful in your recovery?

The survey asked about demographics, education, and family history; the patterns, extent, and consequences of the gambling problem; and recovery steps. The women were also asked to describe in detail what had been most helpful, and to speculate on what they would have liked from helping professionals. Many of the survey questions were open-ended and designed to encourage participants to elaborate on their answers. For example, to the question "What is your meaning of recovery?" one woman referred to a new alertness to life, including "the sound of the woodpecker outside my door." Responses to the open-ended questions are included throughout the book.

It's important to note that the respondents and interviewees do not represent an average group of women who are experiencing or recovering from gambling problems. Rather, they are what's called a "convenience sample" in research terms, that is, they were available and willing to respond. Compared to national averages, these women were better educated, attended more professional treatment and Gamblers Anonymous meetings, and were primarily white and middle-class. However, these attributes did not protect them from gambling's wide-ranging consequences—consequences common to compulsive gamblers regardless of age, income, or race. The respondents reported high gambling debts (on average $46,670), lost jobs, suicide attempts, bad checks and forged checks, bankruptcies, embezzlement, and prison terms, as well as emotional, mental, and physical deterioration. But all these women overcame their addiction's grip, and its devastating consequences, and stopped gambling. I'm happy to report that my friend Sherry is one of these women, and her story is woven into the book with those of the other women I interviewed.

What I learned through the survey forms the core of this book. I can't say that the findings were a great surprise to me, although I didn't go into the project with preconceived notions. I am a professor in my university's school of social work, not an expert in gambling addiction. However, what I did learn was informative and enlightening. The respondents do not represent all female gamblers, nor do their recovery experiences necessarily reflect the latest scientific findings on gambling addiction or best practices in the field. The stories and experiences they described were about how recovery worked for them. As a researcher and as an individual who knew others struggling with problem gambling, I knew it was important to share their stories with others. To that end, their personal histories are the backbone of the book.

From the beginning, academics and professionals in the field of gambling treatment have expressed great interest in the project. My friend Sherry and I were not alone in identifying a gap in knowledge about the recovery process of women with this problem. In 2001, I presented preliminary results at the National Council on Problem Gambling Conference, and in 2002 presented the research findings at a National Conference of Social Work Educators with my colleague Dr. Lisa Avery. Lisa and I also published two journal articles on the research in *Social Work and the Addictions* in 2002 and 2008.

One of the most interesting experiences I had in bringing this research to light was serving as a panelist for the National Center on Addiction and Substance Abuse at a Columbia University conference, "High Stakes: Substance Abuse and Gambling," in June 2001. The distinguished guests on the panels included the CEO of Harrah's casino hotel chain, researchers from Harvard, and Leslie Stahl of CBS News as one of the moderators. I was a little starstruck and, before my panel session, worried about what I could possibly contribute in such company. Then the (male) panel moderator turned to me, looked me directly in the eye, and said, "Now, Dr. Davis . . . is there really something special about women?" I responded very sincerely with "Yes sir, yes, there really is." I relaxed and smiled as the audience laughed, and then explained what was special about women *recovering from compulsive gambling.*

Hope, Hope, and More Hope

This is a book about recovery and hope. But it is also a book about human suffering and the relentless pursuit of some kind of fix for the broken parts of our lives, whether we gamble or not. The purpose of the book is to share the hope of recovery for women everywhere, especially those who are still entrenched in the world of gambling and are feeling very alone.

There has been a significant increase in research on women and compulsive gambling since I conducted my Internet study in 2000 and 2001. This too inspires hope that academia and research are catching up with the reality that women are experiencing gambling problems almost as much as men are. Unfortunately, the research on what works to help people with problem gambling is still very limited. That is why these women's stories, telling what *did* work, need to be shared.

This book also notes some pertinent research findings available in areas that were not covered in the survey. These areas include national trends around women and gambling, factors that may influence a woman's gambling behavior, treatment developments, and ideas to help prevent compulsive gambling.

About This Book

The book has two parts, with chapters that mirror the major sections of the Internet survey. The first part, "The Road to Problem

Gambling," discusses how the survey respondents progressed from recreational to self-destructive gambling. Chapter 1 explores today's realities about women: the rising numbers of female gamblers, why they are so invisible, and how their gambling problems differ from men's. Chapter 2 addresses the question "How could a nice girl like you get hooked on such a self-destructive behavior as compulsive gambling?" Chapter 3 offers questions, cues, and stories to help you consider whether gambling is a problem in your life or the life of a loved one. Chapter 4 describes the costs and consequences of the survey respondents' gambling behavior, and what kinds of experiences helped them to stop.

The purpose of part 2, "Finding Your Way Out: Recovery Options," is to suggest a variety of recovery paths that are grounded both in research and in the real-life experience of the recovering women. It soon becomes clear that although women have some commonalities that affect the context of their addiction and recovery, their personal experience may dictate very different goals, different methods for achieving them, and different measurements of success. This section covers the phenomena of relapse and the bumps along the way to success (chapter 5), Gamblers Anonymous (chapter 6), professional help (chapter 7), what it's like to get well "on your own" (chapter 8), and support from family members and friends (chapter 9). Chapter 10 describes how the women have maintained their recovery through the challenges of their new lives, and some of the rewards of doing just that.

Remember, this is a book about recovery and hope. The purpose is twofold: (1) to share the hope of recovery for women everywhere, especially those who are feeling very alone and still finding their way, and (2) to offer concrete details about how the women actually stopped gambling and built a better life for themselves in recovery. They didn't all do the same thing. Many relied on Gamblers Anonymous for support, but some did not. Some went to professional treatment, but some recovered "on their own." It becomes clear that there are many paths to recovery that can work, and many have common themes. As you meet the women who are traveling these paths, you may discover a way out of your own problem with gambling. A common saying in Twelve Step groups that applies to this book is "Take what you like and leave the rest." Becoming aware of the many women who made it to the other side can spark the hope that begins your own journey to recovery, and the details of how they did it may suggest what steps might work for you.

Although the book is primarily focused on women, there is something here for men as well. Human suffering is not gendered; nor is the relentless pursuit of a fix for the broken part of our lives. Nor is the hope of recovery. The fact that these women took their lives back from what many agree is a "cunning, baffling, and powerful" problem can be a beacon of light for us all.

My heartfelt thanks go to the women who took the time to answer the Internet survey and to the women who allowed me to interview them in more depth. I sincerely hope I have captured the spirit of their inspiring journeys.

PART 1: The Road to Problem Gambling

CHAPTER 1

The Feminization of Gambling

"It's not that we don't like men. It's just that we don't identify with all their issues, and they don't identify with ours." ■■■ **Marilyn, age 72**

This is a book about how to take your life back from compulsive gambling. It is written for women, about women, and based on the real stories of ordinary yet desperate women who succeeded in their efforts to stop gambling. Although the book is written especially for women struggling with compulsive gambling, others are invited and welcome to read on, especially family members of these women, and professionals and academics who want to know more. The primary focus is on women, however. This chapter will explain why.

Women Gamblers: Almost Invisible in Their Misery

You cannot tell by looking at a woman that she has spent all of her last paycheck at the casino the night before, or that she is thinking about how she can feed the kids with no money, or figuring out where she can ask for a loan. Even close family members can be deceived up to a point—and tragically, sometimes that point is suicide. You cannot smell gambling on her breath, and her eyes don't dilate no matter how big her problem is. You won't see much of her in past research studies on gambling, and you will see too little of her in formal treatment programs. You may see her with a roomful of recovering women at a Gamblers Anonymous meeting in a few cities, but in many meetings throughout the country, men will still outnumber her. She may show up at a health clinic with gastrointestinal problems related to uncontrolled gambling, or at a mental health clinic for anxiety or depression, but it is very unlikely she will receive any professional recognition of what's really wrong unless she specifically admits her gambling problems. Even if she does, there is far too little organized treatment, social policy, or research focusing directly on helping women avoid or address compulsive gambling problems.

This book intends to make the problem more visible. Thirty years ago, it was just dawning on the general public and professional treatment programs that women were experiencing alcohol and drug problems, just as men were. A new era finally began, one that included women in research and program development, and that also promoted the more generous understanding that substance addiction is not a moral issue and is treatable. The hidden shame carried by women who were alcoholic or drug addicted diminished as more women went public with the reality of their lives. In the same way, visibility and understanding are critical elements in helping women come forth and get help with their gambling problems. The women in the Internet survey I conducted in 2000 and 2001, although anonymous, have "gone public" through this book—gone public with their real experience of gambling problems and their solutions. An even more important purpose of the book is to offer hope that women *can* and *do* take their lives back from this debilitating problem.

Women Are Gambling as Never Before

But then, so are men. According to a recent national poll, two out of three Americans gambled in the last twelve months.[1] Twenty-five years ago, only Nevada and New Jersey had legalized gambling. Today, nearly 900 casinos are operating in twenty-nine states, state-operated electronic slot machines are available at any bar in Oregon, and every state but Utah and Hawaii has some form of legalized gambling. Some speculate that state governments are now "addicted" to the gambling revenue that produced $20 billion in 2005. Add to that the estimated $13 billion bet online the same year on games such as Texas Hold 'Em and the $22.7 billion in Native American casino revenue,[2] and we get a sense of why the American public is told in countless advertisements that there are so many good reasons to gamble.

How did we come so far and so fast? Some readers of this book will remember the time when legalized gambling was restricted to Nevada (which legalized it in 1931). In the 1960s, state governments were pressured to find more operating money without raising taxes. State-run lotteries began to look more attractive. New Hampshire (1964), New York (1967), and New Jersey (1971) were the beginning of a national trend. Today, thirty-seven states and the District of Columbia have operating lotteries. It is the only form of commercial gambling in the United States that is a government monopoly.

Legal casino gambling in states other than Nevada began developing during the 1970s and 1980s. New Jersey's Atlantic City, a rundown resort area, was revitalized by legal casino gambling beginning in 1978. Native American tribal casinos became legal after the 1987 U.S. Supreme Court decision *California v. Cabazon Band of Mission Indians* ruled that states couldn't regulate commercial gambling on Indian reservations. The next year, Congress passed the Indian Gaming Regulatory Act, which requires tribes to negotiate a gambling compact with the state they reside in. Native American casinos rapidly developed and expanded. According to the National Gambling Impact Study Commission Report (1999), the revenues from tribal gambling grew over thirtyfold from 1988 to 1997, while the revenues from non-tribal casinos merely doubled over the same time period.[3]

Another boost was provided by riverboat casinos, which began operating in Iowa in 1991. By the end of that decade, more than ninety riverboat and dockside casinos were operating on the Mississippi River from Iowa to the state of Mississippi. Part of the draw for riverboat casinos was that they were strategically located to bring in revenues from out-of-state visitors. On top of all this, Internet gambling has become accessible to millions of Americans, and according to the Pew Research Center in 2006, it is the fastest growing segment of the gambling market today. In 2004 alone, Internet gamblers nationwide spent $8 billion on an estimated 1,800 Web sites, and the numbers continue to skyrocket.[4] Although Congress passed the Unlawful Internet Gambling Enforcement Act in October 2006, which prohibited U. S. citizens from using credit cards and bank transfers in Web-based gambling transactions, enforcement has been totally lax. Potential gamblers continue to be lured to sites that make it possible to gamble with alternative types of credit, such as electronic checks, money orders, and credit cards processed in other countries.

The results of the unprecedented increase in gambling venues over the last thirty years are still being argued. In 2004, the economic and social costs of gambling—treatment for addiction, domestic violence, increased crime, bankruptcies, job loss—was estimated by economist Earl Grinols to be $54 billion a year.[5] On the other hand, there are positives: more state funds to pay for goods and services, more job opportunities, and the increased ability of those Native American governments who have developed casinos to enhance opportunity for their tribal members.

Gambling Problems for Women Are Increasing

For most people, gambling does not become a problem. They are the ones who can go to Las Vegas with their kids and truly experience "family entertainment": see the shows, take advantage of the cheap buffets, and spend a limited amount of money on the slot machines. If they happen to win anything, they are likely to go home and brag about it instead of putting all the winnings back into the machine. However, according to the National Research Council, gambling does become problematic for about 3 to 7 percent of those who gambled in the past year.[6]

These estimates have been criticized as being too low because many researchers rely on telephone interviews for their surveys. A problem gambler is more likely to be in a casino or card room than at home evenings and weekends answering a telephone survey. If the problem is bad enough, she's unlikely to even have a phone. And such a person is likely to minimize the problem, especially talking to a stranger. But the gambling industry benefits when the problem is underestimated: it can make a case for expanding gambling, blame problems on the weakness of a few individuals, and ignore the social costs.

On the whole, men are more likely to be pathological, problem, or at-risk gamblers, but women are catching up fast. Men and women gamble at almost the same rate in areas where slot machines or video poker machines are located in restaurants, grocery stores, hotels, or places readily accessible to women. For example, in three states where electronic gaming machines are easily accessible, close to half of all problem and pathological gamblers are women: 51 percent in Montana (1998), 50 percent in Louisiana (1999), and 45 percent in Oregon (2000). Nor is the trend restricted to the

United States. In Australia, the rate of women problem gamblers rose from 14 to 41 percent between 1991 and 1999.[7]

Evidence from various state telephone Helpline surveys also suggests that women have been calling for help with increasing frequency. The Arizona Council on Compulsive Gambling reports that women make about 60 percent of its Helpline calls, [8] and the Connecticut Council on Problem Gambling reports a 31 to 37 percent increase in Helpline calls from women from 1996 to 2002.[9]

Gambling for Women: Acceptable as a Pastime, Still Unacceptable as a Problem

Historically, gambling was the province of men. As recently as the 1970s, men dominated the racetracks, off-track betting sites, sports betting, and card games, as well as the casinos in Atlantic City and Nevada. The old "know when to hold 'em, know when to fold 'em" image of male gamblers coexisted with the popular cultural notion that men were the risk-takers. Respectable middle-class women were seen as caretakers and keepers of the hearth, and more likely to show up at charity bingos.

The unprecedented expansion of legal gambling opportunities throughout the United States changed all that in the last thirty years. Gambling has been sanitized into "gaming" and has become much more attractive to women: many venues provide a safe place for women to come alone. Accessibility, perks, and amenities have improved. Some casinos now offer day care and hourly babysitting for children as young as six weeks old, fun centers for children, and full-service spas.

Two other dramatic trends in recent decades have impacted the way women are perceived in relation to gambling. Cultural ideas about a "woman's place" became less potent with the rapid increase of women in the American workplace. In addition, almost every state now uses some form of gambling revenue to shore up its budgets. To reach their goals, state governments are framing gambling as a civic function to help build schools; no longer is it off limits for a "respectable" woman.

Although the current culture is more approving of women gambling in general, negative attitudes persist about women with problems in this area. When a woman is gambling instead of fulfilling her cultural role of homemaker, mother, caretaker, or employee, society does not approve. Neither does the woman herself, who holds the same societal values. The women who responded to the 2000–2001 Internet survey expressed a great deal of shame and regret over their inability to carry on their female roles while in the midst of their gambling problems. When asked what they regret the most, many noted the impact on their families:

- "Gambling robbed me of my soul, values, and I caused my family to worry about me."
- "I caused my family so much mental anguish, especially my son."
- "I lost me, and I lost so much time with my children."
- "I most regret hurting my husband, and the lies I have told him about the money."

While men may certainly experience similar regrets, they are more likely to focus on financial losses than relationship losses. Women in the Internet survey, while also experiencing financial ruin, reported that losing the ability to connect emotionally to family and friends is even more devastating.

Women's Issues Differ from Men's

As Marilyn, an Internet survey participant, puts it: "It's not that we don't like men. It's just that we don't identify with all their issues, and they don't identify with ours." One big difference is that women have a historical economic disadvantage. Some researchers suggest this plays a part in a woman's motivation to gamble: the possibility of winning money that she has no other way to earn or acquire can be a powerful incentive.

Casinos are especially attractive to women because they are relatively safe for women who are alone, and they provide a temporary escape from bad moods, boredom, and loneliness. Casinos are among the very few places where women in this culture can go by themselves and experience safety, anonymity, and social approval.

Gambling is a way for some women to rebel against feminine duties and obligations. An addiction therapist (female) who works full-time with problem gamblers explores this idea:

> ■ ■ ■ *Almost every female client I have seen states that gambling is in some manner a way of her "letting go of her obligations;" "rebelling;" "doing what I want, finally, after taking care of everyone else all my life." Many of my clients have experienced abusive relationships and lasting loneliness. Several are grandmothers, many are divorced, and a few are young and with partners. The crux of this rebellion seems to be the end result of feeling emotionally and physically responsible to others first and themselves last. When the pressure cap finally blows, and the woman says, "Screw you, world, watch me do what I want!" she finds herself "asserting" her autonomy in a casino or bingo game, etc.*[10] ■ ■ ■

For some women, gambling can be a weapon of power and revenge. A study of women who gamble in the Canadian province of Ontario found that 28 percent of them reported financial abuse from their partner, and 24 percent admitted to "setting aside money my partner doesn't know about." Half of the 365 women surveyed responded that being able "to do what I want with my money" was a reason for gambling.[11]

Other gender disparities show up when people enter professional treatment: women report more physical neglect, more emotional and sexual abuse, and are more likely to be depressed and experience anxiety. Indeed, in many areas of life, women's experience differs from that of men, so it makes sense that they experience gambling problems and the challenges of recovery differently as well.

Information on Women and Gambling Is Scant

Because women with gambling problems were nowhere to be found in research studies at that time, it became clear to me that there was a big hole in the information available to women who were caught in that cycle and wanted to find a way out. Upon learning of my friend Sherry's problem in 2000, I went to several mainstream bookstores and found very little on compulsive gambling, and nothing focused on women. In one store, I was directed to the section that featured books on how to win at poker and slots! Thankfully, there are now more research studies that include women. But we still lack real first-person accounts of how women are actually stopping problem gambling. That's where this book comes in.

CHAPTER 2

Getting Hooked

"We liked the free perks we got from them, we loved the free dinners, the free gifts; if you had enough points you could get a gift, and we had free turkeys." ▪▪▪ **Irma, age 65**

T he road to compulsive gambling begins innocently. A common refrain in many Twelve Step groups is that "I didn't grow up dreaming of becoming a member of *this* organization." Many women in the Internet survey, just like Irma, liked to go gambling for the free perks, socializing with their friends, or just a night out. Most started later in life and had never gambled previously, or only at occasional bingo games or a trip to Las Vegas. Some commented they didn't even like gambling, prior to the experience of "getting hooked." When they did start to experiment with it, they tended to go to casinos in groups with family or friends. They also limited the amount of money lost and stuck to it, and they "had fun" while they were there. How does this kind of harmless fun turn into the monster of compulsive gambling? When does the line get crossed?

Susan believes that her initial "innocent" experience with gambling had the seeds of the problems to come. As she describes it:

▪▪▪ *I had never been to a casino until I was forty-nine. And I went with my sister and we got over there and I didn't realize but I had an abscessed tooth. And I stayed up all night; I didn't even know how to play. But I managed to take my forty dollars and stay up all night long. As long as I played, my tooth didn't hurt. I didn't really spend more money than I had planned or anything like that. But I think that's probably when my brain registered that this takes away the pain. So we left, and that was that. I didn't have a desire to go back or even think about gambling.* ▪▪▪

But of course Susan did go back, at the invitation of a wealthy relative who gave everyone money to go to the casino as part of a birthday celebration. During this second episode, she recalls, "My money went just like that and I remember just going back and getting more money and not telling anybody, pretending I was still spending the same money."

What is it that caused Susan to hide her losses at this early stage? Why did she go from no "desire to go back or even think about gambling" to very problematic behavior in a matter of a few months? We simply don't know the exact cause. However, we do know that certain personal and environmental factors are associated with problem gambling. Some might call these "risk factors" because they describe vulnerabilities in a person's life or conditions in the environment that make gambling an attractive choice at the time.

Personal factors often associated with problem gambling include:

1. *Coping problems.* Gambling is a potent escape from emotional pain, boredom, or new problems that seem overwhelming, like the death of a spouse, retirement, or divorce.
2. *Coexisting problems.* There is a higher incidence of gambling problems with women who currently or in the past have had alcohol or drug problems. Anxiety and depression are more frequent with women problem gamblers than men.
3. *Brain problems.* Emerging research suggests that there may be several ways in which the brains of compulsive gamblers are vulnerable to the stimulating environment of the casino.

Environmental problems, that is, external factors that increase risk, include:

1. *Location, location, location.* Proximity to a casino is linked with problem gambling.
2. *Technology traps.* Casinos are carefully designed to overwhelm, comfort, overstimulate, and seduce people not only to gamble, but to gamble longer than they planned. Although the technology traps exist for all patrons of the casino, they may be more potent for a person who has some of the individual vulnerability factors described above.

Now let's look at each of these factors in more detail.

Personal Risk Factors

Although winning money seems like a common-sense reason to gamble, this may not be the major motivation.[1] Gambling is a potent escape from pain, boredom, and the everyday problems of life. Many of the women in the Internet study attest to its power to completely wipe out their worries or concerns. As Julie says, "When I'm sitting in front of the Sun and Moon [slot] machine and I'm putting in yet another hundred-dollar bill, I'm completely focused. There is nothing or no one that will distract me. I put off going to the bathroom as long as I possibly can."

Coping Problems

When asked "What reason influenced you to start gambling seriously?" many women reported seeking a temporary escape from painful events and situations. These included:

- "death of a brother"
- "death of a best friend"
- "a grown son with drug and mental problems"
- "teenage son using drugs, running away, etc."
- "in debt and the money I did have never seemed to go far enough"

■ "problems with adult children and grandchildren"
■ "severe symptoms of anxiety disorder"
■ "depression"

As one woman explained, "For me, sitting for hours at slot machines is the ultimate drug of escape."

Historically, problem gamblers were conveniently seen as either the "action" type (primarily males) or the "escape" type (primarily females). Consistent with prevailing gender stereotypes, action gamblers preferred games of "skill" and judgment such as poker, horse racing, and sports, while escape gamblers preferred "non-skill" games such as electronic slot machines. But as more and more women bet on so-called "skill" games, and more and more men play electronic slot machines and Internet games, this stereotypical division is fading. For example, the Arizona Council on Compulsive Gambling reports that in 1999, 49 percent of its male hotline callers met its criteria for "escape gamblers."[2]

Why do women begin "serious" gambling? The top reason reported on the Internet study was boredom, followed by escaping negative feelings or experiences (loneliness, depression, worries about spouses, jobs, finances) and seeking positive experiences (looking for action, fun, a big win, "I just loved it!"). It's clear there are many reasons women feel compelled to gamble, even when the negative consequences are piling up.

Coexisting Problems

What kind of problems might drive a woman to escape through gambling even at the cost of self-destruction? Several research studies indicate that women with gambling problems are more likely than their male counterparts to have problems such as depression and anxiety as well. Joanne recalls a conversation with her doctor, which illustrates the need for follow-up questions about these issues: "The doctor asked me, how often do you get depressed? I said only about twice a year, and she asked, for how long? I said about six months."

Both women and men gamblers frequently have substance abuse or dependence, and attention-deficit/hyperactivity disorder (ADHD) as well.[3] Not only are problem gamblers at increased risk for other psychiatric disorders, many have already experienced significant troubles in other areas of their lives. In a recent study on the rate of childhood maltreatment in pathological gamblers, women reported higher rates than men in overall rates of maltreatment as well as emotional abuse, physical neglect, and sexual abuse.[4] In addition, the researchers found that childhood maltreatment is associated with the onset and severity of gambling problems.

Research surveys find that compulsive gamblers tend to have family members with high rates of similar problems. Studies show that up to 43 percent of compulsive gamblers have a parent with a serious alcohol or drug problem, and up to 28 percent have a parent who was probably a compulsive gambler.[5] In the Internet study, the combined rate of alcoholism and drug addiction problems in the women's families was 80 percent, serious depression or bipolar disorder was a problem in 63 percent, and gambling was a serious problem in 59 percent. ("Families" included spouse or partner, siblings, parents, grandparents, aunts, and uncles.) As one woman explained: "Mom and Dad were compulsive gamblers. Need I say more?"

More than a quarter (28 percent) of the women reported a lifetime personal history of addiction to either alcohol or drugs. Of those, over half (60 percent) said they were clean and sober *before* they experienced their problems with gambling. Altogether, 41 percent of the women reported a history of mental illness, primarily depression, bipolar disorder, or dysthymia. [6]

While it is clear that women who have problems with gambling are likely to have many additional troubles in their lives, we don't yet know how these factors are related. For example, many have experienced childhood maltreatment, family disorders, and unhappiness, but this fact does not prove that such problems *cause* or *lead to* compulsive gambling. What we do know is that addressing these issues may be critical to getting on, and staying on, the road of recovery.

Brain Problems

Some intriguing new research suggests that the brains of compulsive gamblers may have a higher-than-average vulnerability to developing gambling problems. At a 2005 conference on the prevention, research, and treatment of problem gambling, Dr. Jon Grant, an expert on impulse-control disorders, described the essence of these complex research findings in layman's terms.[7] According to Dr. Grant, several features are "a little out of whack" in the brains of compulsive gamblers. The functioning of serotonin, a chemical neurotransmitter in the brain that can help to regulate mood, is "a little off" compared to people who don't have a gambling addiction. Dopamine and endorphins—chemicals that reward us and tell us when something feels good—are also out of whack. Dr. Grant notes that certain medications that affect these chemicals, such as bupropion (Wellbutrin) and naltrexone, have been found helpful in reducing gambling addiction.

In the area of impulse control, the part of the brain that tells us "Don't do it!" is less activated in people who have a gambling addiction. Although research has established that *something* is different in the brains of compulsive gamblers, Dr. Grant emphasizes that we don't yet understand which comes first—the addiction or the brain differences. And we don't yet have the specific treatments to start returning the brain to normal functioning.

Other intriguing brain research finds that dopamine transmission is most active in situations where reward is uncertain. In other

words, the *anticipation* of a reward may be the strongest trigger
for a dopamine rush. Since the results of gambling are always uncertain, the dopamine activity may continue to reinforce the behavior regardless of the outcome.[8] This may help explain why near
misses are so thrilling. Even if you don't get what you want, picking up that last card that *may* be the missing ace, or watching the
slot machine numbers drop after you've already pulled two sevens,
can get the dopamine surging. It also helps explain why gambling
is so hard to stop. Your brain wants you to be "in action," that is,
in a position to anticipate and get the dopamine rush, regardless of
whether you are winning or losing.

Emerging research on the brain is yielding many other findings that relate to compulsive gambling.[9] Through neuroimaging
techniques, pictures of brain mechanisms show abnormalities in
the brain function of pathological gamblers, similar to those ob-
served in other addictions. For example, in one study, compulsive gamblers had deficits in their brain's ability to shift attention
and a diminished capacity to weigh in negative consequences. The
focus of such a brain is on how to reduce the built-up tension,
not on what that action will cost. Other studies indicate that in
this respect, the brain pathways of compulsive gamblers are very
similar to drug addicts' in that they both focus on the need for
tension reduction. Impulsivity—the need to act now regardless of
consequences—is common to both substance abusers and compulsive gamblers, but gamblers are even more impulsive.

How does the brain interact with the casino environment?
Think of what happens when you win a jackpot. The excitement
of "Jackpot!" becomes even bigger with sounds of bells and whis-
tles, the attention of several casino staff, the envious stares of by-
standers, and the slap of crisp hundred-dollar bills laid on your
outstretched hand. It is ironic that the "reward" of gambling is the
very thing that can program your brain to keep on gambling, in

spite of the consequences. This is because the surge of dopamine that occurs with a big win makes us feel very good. Thus, we are encouraged to continue the behavior that brought us to that high level of pleasure. In addition, scientists have discovered that the experience of an emotional high such as a jackpot is encoded in a special place in the brain where it becomes a "privileged" memory. This may account for the vivid recall of jackpots and the not-so-clear memory of loss after loss after loss.[10]

A few big wins can accelerate a gambling problem. Although the experience is different for every woman, most can easily recall the euphoria of those early wins. Mary remembers her first win as if in Technicolor. She says, "The first time I sat down to the slot machines I won eight hundred dollars. And within about half an hour I won a thousand dollars. And I thought—oh, this is great. I think I have those machines figured out." For Sarah, the experience of a first win was almost accidental, but it started her on the road to compulsive gambling. As she describes it, "Waiting for my husband to get off the phone in a convenience store (where there was a line of slot machines), I asked somebody to teach me how to play, won ten dollars, and played (compulsively) for two years after that." Brenda, who eventually went to prison because of her gambling, remembers, "When I was about forty-five years old, I got the chance to go to Reno for a bowling tournament. I didn't care about gambling, but I went into a couple of casinos, and when I played the slot machines I was very lucky and I won something on almost every machine." Alas, for these women, the good times stopped very soon.

It is not within the scope of this book to detail the intricacies of the brain research studies cited above; however, if the reader wants to know more, the 2007 text *Stress and Addiction: Biological and Psychological Mechanisms,* edited by Mustafa al'Absi, is recommended. There is a chapter devoted to how dopamine works in the brain, as well as a chapter on impulsive behaviors that includes brain research on pathological gambling. Another helpful book on impulse control disorders, including gambling, is *Stop Me Because I Can't Stop Myself: Taking Control of Impulsive Behavior* (2003), by Jon E. Grant and S. W. Kim.

Environmental Risk Factors

Now let's consider the external influences that can accelerate a gambling problem.

Location, Location, Location

A person needs access to a gambling venue in order to gamble and, Internet betting aside, living close to such a venue can be a risk factor. The National Gambling Impact Study Commission Report (1999) found that a gambling facility within fifty miles roughly doubles the prevalence of problem and pathological gamblers in an area.[11] However, some researchers pose the question, which came first? Do people who are already problem gamblers flock to a new, convenient casino or does the new, convenient casino attract people who then start having problems with gambling?

Sally's experience supports the findings of the Commission Report. Other than card games with her family growing up, and very occasional trips to Reno with her husband, gambling was not a part of her life. When a casino was built only fifteen miles from her town, she and her friends started going out there about once a month for "something new to do." Gambling was still on the margins of her life; she had a good job, a husband, and two children still in school. However, the food at the casino tasted good, the price was good, it was "kinda exciting," and eventually the gambling was good. "I will never forget my first jackpot," she says. "After all those times of losing my forty-dollar limit, I finally connected, and it felt *great*." She started going back to the casino without her girlfriends, convinced she could win more. The casino was so close she could gamble over a long lunch hour or after work when she "had to stay late for a so-called project." As the months went by, Sally found more and more reasons to be away from her family. "I lied to my husband, my kids, my in-laws, my employer, my friends, everybody," she says. "I was spending every single possible minute I could at the casino. It was just too easy; in fifteen minutes I could be sitting in front of my favorite machine, getting my fix, and it was all legal!"

It makes sense that living near a casino or card room is a risk factor simply because it makes it easier to get to where you'll be gambling. In the same way, the hours that casinos keep—most are open seven days a week, twenty-four hours a day—has also been associated with the development of pathological gambling.[12] When asked to name the hardest part of the recovery process for them, several women in the Internet survey mentioned their proximity to casinos and the advertising associated with them. For example:

- "The desire is triggered because gambling is everywhere you go."
- "The advertising, television, radio, and billboards are everywhere—it makes it hard to stay with my commitment to stop."
- "It's as though every channel of TV is advertising this casino and that casino, and it does get to you."
- "Three casinos have been put up in my area in the past year and a half. That doesn't make my urges any easier."
- "Passing the card rooms on the way home from work every morning (I work nights), when I'm wide awake and have the whole day in front of me. I think of how nice it would be to just 'stop in' for a 'few hands,' but I know I'll never leave."

Technology Traps

Modern casinos are carefully designed to overwhelm, over-stimulate, comfort, and seduce people not only to gamble, but to gamble longer than they planned. At the top of the list are the devices used to convince the customer that the casino is an exciting place to be. All the clanging bells, blaring songs, flashing lights, and sirens are part of the behavior modification techniques that increase a person's state of arousal prior to or during the actual gambling episode. Behavior modification specialists are clear that such a "secondary" arousal can become just as attractive and rewarding as the actual play of gambling. Thus, for a person addicted to gambling, the pleasurable experience begins upon entering a casino and hearing the tinkling music from the slot machines, the shouts from the craps tables, and the clicking of poker chips.

Video poker and electronic slot machines are the most popular form of gambling both for women in general and for the women in the Internet survey. These types of machines have characteristics that are linked to the development of gambling problems: a very rapid rate of play (as many as fifteen games a minute, or 900 per hour), repetitive play that can produce a trancelike state, and the illusion of control.[13] Gambling establishments promote this illusion by allowing customers to choose the size of the bet, rewarding payouts on bonus games based on the customer picking the right option, and varying the casino payout rate on different slot machines to encourage customers to choose the right machine.

Other behavioral techniques of video poker and electronic slot machines that reinforce the customer to keep betting include:

- *Winner!!!* Extraordinary visual displays and special sounds and music reinforce wins immediately. Sarah says the music associated with a particular slot machine stayed with her for days, and she had to work hard to "turn off my brain."
- Just when you think the machine is "cold," up pops a winning combination. This technique reinforces continuous play, regardless of how much you are losing. Randomly spaced

rewards that you can't predict comprise the strongest form of operant conditioning, and it is the most difficult type of conditioning to break.

- "I just know it's trying to hit . . ." Frequent near misses and small wins give the illusion of future rewards. Loss periods are brief, even though the wins are small, so there is no time or inclination to contemplate losses.

- Winnings can be put back into the machine and gambled immediately. No need to stand in the long line at the cashier station when you could be winning more!

- Seats are engineered for comfort; there are no hard edges coming into contact with main arteries and possibly putting your leg asleep, causing you to get up and leave the machine.

- "Hi Susie!" Membership cards let you know you are "special" as they pop up on the machine and welcome you by name.

- What time is it, anyway? Lack of reference points such as clocks or windows promotes a sense of timelessness that makes it easier to lose awareness of yourself and your responsibilities in real life.

Another type of manipulation occurs in state lotteries: "The Mega Jackpot is up to $10 million!" we might be told. State lottery commissions take advantage of another powerful incentive by structuring lotteries to reflect people's attraction to bets featuring large rewards, even if there is a small chance of winning that award. According to the National Gambling Impact Study Commission, Oregon and Arizona modified their lotteries several times to lower the odds of winning and provide a bigger jackpot in order to successfully increase betting behavior.[14]

The manipulation of the psyche is part of every marketing strategy in the gambling industry. The techniques described above only scratch the surface of the sophisticated technology developed to lure people to gamble, and to keep gambling. They are so powerful that even becoming aware of them is not enough to keep you from being entranced. Although the technology traps apply to everyone who enters a casino, they may be particularly potent for those people who have some of the personal risk factors mentioned above. That's probably why Gamblers Anonymous (GA) literature advises, "Don't go in or near gambling establishments" when you are trying to stop.[15]

You Don't Have to Be Problem-Free to Stop Gambling

All this information about casinos' manipulation techniques, and the vulnerabilities that seem to go with gambling problems, may seem discouraging. What if you have most or even all the personal and environmental problems? A hopeless approach to this information could even feed into what some women have used as another excuse to gamble: "Why bother quitting? I'm doomed anyway."

This is where the information from the Internet survey gives us *hope*. Most of the women in the study did have these kinds of problems. They were also under the influence of the manipulations of the casinos, just like everyone else. Yet they stopped gambling in spite of all this!

They had to work hard in their recovery to deal with some of their other issues, through professional treatment, counselors, GA sponsors, and the support of their families. When you're gambling, problems with marriage and family, depression, and so on, are not at the forefront of your mind, even though they continue to percolate. You are mainly focused on how to cover your losses and get more money to gamble. When the gambling stops, you can get help for these kinds of personal problems at last. You begin to understand what they are, and because you're not gambling, you have the strength to look at them instead of futilely trying to escape them.

Before we trace more specifically how gambling took over the lives of the women in the Internet survey, let's pause in the next chapter to explore how to determine whether your own gambling habits are problematic.

CHAPTER 3

Is My Gambling a Problem?

"Gambling was not my problem. My problem was losing too much money. Then my problem became losing too much money, and losing too much time away from my job and family. Then my problem became losing my car, and then the house, and maybe even my family. Finally, my problem became gambling." ▪▪▪ **Julie, age 43**

As Julie says, it is usually the consequences of gambling behavior that finally hammers home the idea that gambling itself is a problem. Most people don't recognize their addictive behavior is a problem and don't give it up until meaningful consequences are occurring or threatening to occur. Screening instruments to assess whether a gambling problem exists generally use consequences as a yardstick. In this chapter, we'll examine some informal and formal screening instruments so that you can take a more careful look at your own gambling habits, if that is helpful. We will begin with less formal assessments, including the Gamblers Anonymous Twenty Questions, before moving on to the most common screening instruments used to formally assess problem gambling. We'll also hear the stories of other women who decided for themselves that they were in trouble with gambling. The chapter's last section focuses on how families and concerned friends might discover that gambling is the problem that has shut them out of their loved ones' lives.

First, let's take a closer look at the language used to describe problem gambling.

If It Is a Problem, What Should I Call It?

There is no agreement yet in either the scientific or popular literature about the specific differences between problem, compulsive, and pathological gambling. The distinctions depend on the beliefs and values of various constituencies. In general, "pathological gambling" is a more scientific term defined by the National Research Council as a "mental disorder characterized by a continuous or periodic loss of control over gambling, a preoccupation with gambling, and with obtaining money with which to gamble, irrational thinking, and a continuation of the behavior despite adverse consequences."[1] A more blunt description from the same National Research Council report and based on clinical evidence is that "pathological gamblers engage in destructive behaviors: they commit crimes, they run up large debts, they damage relationships with family and friends, and they kill themselves."[2] A clinical diagnosis of pathological gambling is reached when a person meets five or more of the *Diagnostic and Statistical Manual of Mental Disorders* criteria, which are described in detail on pages 33–34.[3]

"Problem gambling" is a category generally used in research studies to indicate people who have developed some family, work, or financial problems because of their gambling, but haven't met at least five of the criteria. It is also applied to adolescents, regardless of their scores on various assessment instruments, because of a reluctance to label them as "pathological" while in the midst of fluctuating and experimental behavior patterns. Often the general term "problem gamblers" is used inclusively to indicate both pathological and problem gamblers—a general category also referred to as "disordered gambling."

The designation "compulsive gambler" is a layman's term for "pathological gambler." It is the preferred term in GA, and is used more frequently in general public arenas. According to GA, a compulsive gambler is someone who will answer yes to at least seven of the twenty questions on its screening tool (see pages 31–32).

Informal Screening

One of the nicest things about Twelve Step groups such as Gamblers Anonymous and Alcoholics Anonymous is that the members don't tell you whether or not you have a problem. It's your job to figure it out. It doesn't matter how many signs you have of the problem, or whether an expert has diagnosed you with the problem: it's your responsibility to decide if you want to quit gambling for whatever reason makes sense to you. The advantage of this approach is that when you do figure it out, you don't have to rebel against someone else telling you that you have a problem. Here's the story of Irma, who figured it out for herself:

■■■ *My husband moved out in 1992, and then I had knee surgery, and then I started to get a little better and I started thinking I was lonely. I had a girlfriend that liked to gamble, so we went down to the casino in the boats. That was 1995, and I was sixty-five years old. And I did enjoy gambling: it was very fun. We liked all the perks we got from them, we loved the free dinners, the free gifts—if you had enough points you would get a gift, and we had free turkeys. By 1997, I was going by myself, staying overnight at the casino, staying there for hours, doing the chasing, thinking that I could get my money back. Oh, it just got so bad I was going to jump off the bridge into the river. That's when I called the 1-800 number for help.* ■■■

Even if you're not at the "jump off the bridge" stage, you may still be visiting the casino more often than you'd like. Here is what one woman noticed about problem gamblers in action:

▪▪▪ *Women who are problem gamblers are easy to spot in a casino. They never look up when I pass behind them, even if I accidentally bump them because of the close quarters around some of the slot machines and blackjack tables. Many smoke. Many are over fifty, but there are young and intense women too. They don't eat; they don't even take bathroom breaks if they can help it. I know one woman whose bladder was completely distended by the time she got in recovery and it took a year to get back to normal. They usually come by themselves . . . this is not group fun. They rarely smile, even when they win a big jackpot. They are not the ones that jump up and down and yell when they get "lucky." They just go on to the next game. And on . . . and on, until they have lost every last dollar of their "win." They are usually acquainted with the drink and change people, and security. You can see them say a few words, bantering back and forth about "how it's going" tonight, even asking about their kids.*

You often meet up with them at the check line and the cash machines—until the cashier won't cash any more checks, and the cash machine says the dreaded Transaction Denied. *Then they walk quickly, trying not to look at anybody, across the casino into the mostly empty parking lot at four or five in the morning, and try to figure out how they got there once again. If they are like me, they are too numb to even cry. Instead, they pound the steering wheel and yell and cuss at themselves, or simply sit there and wonder how they will ever make it through the drive home and the day ahead.* ▪▪▪

These are the kinds of stories and observations that are routinely told at Gamblers Anonymous meetings. Often, just hearing other people's stories can tell you if you are in the right place and can help you make a self-assessment. If you figure out that gambling is negatively affecting your life in any way, and you want to stop altogether, then you are qualified for membership in GA. Each person has the right to his or her own "bottom" or stopping place. For some, it came when they found themselves five hundred dollars in debt and still couldn't stop. For others, it came when they were headed for prison. Determining whether you want to stop gambling is up to you. GA states that "people seek help when they have reached a personal low in their lives, and only the individual sufferer knows when that point has been reached."[4]

GA's list of Twenty Questions, usually read aloud at every meeting, can help people decide for themselves if they are compulsive gamblers. According to GA, most compulsive gamblers will answer yes to at least seven of the questions.

GA's Twenty Questions[5]

1. Did you ever lose time from work or school due to gambling?
2. Has gambling ever made your home life unhappy?
3. Did gambling affect your reputation?
4. Have you ever felt remorse after gambling?
5. Did you ever gamble to get money with which to pay debts or otherwise solve financial difficulties?
6. Did gambling cause a decrease in your ambition or efficiency?
7. After losing did you feel you must return as soon as possible and win back your losses?
8. After a win did you have a strong urge to return and win more?

The Gamblers Anonymous Twenty Questions are reprinted from the official Gamblers Anonymous Web site, www.gamblersanonymous.org, with permission.

9. *Did you often gamble until your last dollar was gone?*
10. *Did you ever borrow to finance your gambling?*
11. *Have you ever sold anything to finance gambling?*
12. *Were you reluctant to use "gambling money" for normal expenditures?*
13. *Did gambling make you careless of the welfare of yourself or your family?*
14. *Did you ever gamble longer than you had planned?*
15. *Have you ever gambled to escape worry or trouble?*
16. *Have you ever committed, or considered committing, an illegal act to finance gambling?*
17. *Did gambling cause you to have difficulty in sleeping?*
18. *Do arguments, disappointments or frustrations create within you an urge to gamble?*
19. *Did you ever have an urge to celebrate any good fortune by a few hours of gambling?*
20. *Have you ever considered self-destruction or suicide as a result of your gambling?*

Self-described compulsive gamblers, not professional treatment providers or researchers, developed these twenty questions. Although most GA members answer yes to many more than seven of them, the exact number doesn't matter. If you are experiencing any negative consequences from your gambling, if you are having trouble walking away from it, and if you want to stop, you will be welcome at GA.

Like Gamblers Anonymous, a few researchers have advocated for the right of women to define their own gambling problems, instead of being diagnosed and put into some formal category such as "pathological gambler." In 1997, feminist researchers Sarah Brown and Louise Coventry launched the "Queen of Hearts" research project in Australia. They interviewed hundreds of women gamblers and concluded that instead of focusing on an individual diagnosis that invokes the label of "deviant," it is more important for women to make their own evaluation of the problem based on their perceived level of control. The research team also examined the structural and social context that influences gambling behavior, such as the fact that women are generally poorer than men and have fewer pathways to financial success. They included life-cycle factors, family relationships, and cultural values in their analysis—factors that are generally ignored in most screening and diagnostic instruments.[6] Instead of narrowly focusing on just the gambling behavior, Brown and Coventry advocated helping women make changes that were meaningful to their lives as a whole.

Formal Screening

The *Diagnostic and Statistical Manual of Mental Disorders (DSM)* was developed by professionals from the American Psychiatric Association to provide common definitions of mental problems for mental health clinicians and insurance companies. The revised fourth edition (known as the *DSM-IV-TR*) offers a definition of pathological gambling that is widely used in the United States to qualify people for entering outpatient and inpatient treatment, therapy, and when covered, insurance payments. A clinical diagnosis is reached when a person meets five or more of the following criteria:

1. Preoccupation with gambling
2. A need to gamble with increasing amounts of money
3. Restlessness or irritability when attempting to cut down or stop gambling
4. Returning another day to try to get even after losing money ("chasing")
5. Making repeated unsuccessful efforts to quit

6. Gambling to escape problems or bad moods
7. Lying to conceal the extent of gambling
8. Jeopardizing or losing a significant relationship, job, or educational activity because of gambling
9. Committing illegal acts (forgery, fraud, embezzlement) to finance gambling
10. Borrowing money to pay debts[7]

In addition to using the *DSM-IV-TR* criteria for diagnosing pathological gambling, many treatment professionals use the South Oaks Gambling Screen (SOGS) to screen women and men for pathological gambling.[8] This sixteen-item screen is widely used in research and epidemiological studies and has good reliability and validity in clinical work. The clinical cutoff score for "probable pathological gambler" is five. The severity of the problem is commonly assessed by the number of yes answers, and by considering time spent and money lost gambling.

The screening tool and scoring directions are reprinted here. The SOGS may be reproduced as long as the language is used as printed and the scored items are not revised without permission of the author.

South Oaks Gambling Screen[9]

1. Please indicate which of the following types of gambling you have done in your lifetime. For each type, mark one answer: "not at all," "less than once a week," or "once a week or more."

	Not at all	Less than once a week	Once a week or more
a. played cards for money			
b. bet on horses, dogs, or other animals (off-track betting, at the track, or with a bookie)			
c. bet on sports (parlay cards, with a bookie, or at Jai Alai court)			
d. played dice games (including craps, over & under, or other dice games) for money or drinks, etc.			
e. gambled in a casino (legal or otherwise)			
f. played the numbers or bet the lotteries			
g. played bingo for money			
h. played the stock, options, and/ or commodities markets			
i. played slot machines, poker machines, or other game of skill for money			
j. played pull tabs or "paper" games other than lotteries			
k. other forms of gambling not listed above			

2. What is the largest amount of money you have ever gambled with on any one day?

- ☐ Never have gambled
- ☐ $1 or less
- ☐ More than $1, up to $10
- ☐ More than $10, up to $100
- ☐ More than $100, up to $1,000
- ☐ More than $1,000, up to $10,000
- ☐ More than $10,000

3. Check which of the following people in your life has (or had) a gambling problem.

- ☐ Father
- ☐ Mother
- ☐ A brother-in-law
- ☐ A grandparent
- ☐ My spouse or partner
- ☐ My child(ren)
- ☐ Another relative
- ☐ A friend or someone else important in my life

4. When you gamble, how often do you go back another day to win back the money you lost?

- ☐ Never
- ☐ Some of the time (less than half of the time I lost)
- ☐ Most of the time I lost
- ☐ Every time I lost

5. Have you ever claimed to be winning money gambling but were not really? In fact, you lost?

- ☐ Never
- ☐ Yes, most of the time
- ☐ Yes, less than half the time I lost

6. Do you feel you have ever had a problem with betting money or gambling?

- ☐ No
- ☐ Yes
- ☐ Yes, in the past but not now

7. Did you ever gamble more than you intended to?

- ☐ No
- ☐ Yes

8. Have people criticized your betting or told you that you had a gambling problem, regardless of whether or not you thought it was true?

- ☐ No
- ☐ Yes

9. Have you ever felt guilty about the way you gamble or what happens when you gamble?

- ☐ No
- ☐ Yes

10. Have you ever felt like you would like to stop betting money or gambling but didn't think you could?

- ☐ No
- ☐ Yes

11. Have you ever hidden betting slips, lottery tickets, gambling money, IOUs, or other signs of betting or gambling from your spouse, children, or other important people in your life?

- ☐ No
- ☐ Yes

12. Have you ever argued with people you live with over how you handle money?

  ☐ No
  ☐ Yes

13. (If you answered yes to question 12): Have money arguments ever centered around your gambling?

  ☐ No
  ☐ Yes

14. Have you ever borrowed from someone and not paid them back as a result of your gambling?

  ☐ No
  ☐ Yes

15. Have you ever lost time from work (or school) due to gambling?

  ☐ No
  ☐ Yes

16. If you borrowed money to gamble or to pay gambling debts, who or where did you borrow from?

No	Yes	
☐	☐	a. From household money
☐	☐	b. From your spouse
☐	☐	c. From other relatives or in-laws
☐	☐	d. From banks, loan companies, or credit unions
☐	☐	e. From credit cards
☐	☐	f. From loan sharks
☐	☐	g. I cashed in stocks, bonds, life insurance, or other securities
☐	☐	h. I sold personal or family property
☐	☐	i. I borrowed on my checking account (passed bad checks)

☐ ☐ j. I have (had) a credit line with a bookie

☐ ☐ k. I have (had) a credit line with a casino

Score Sheet for SOGS

Scores on the SOGS are determined by scoring one point for each question that shows the "at risk" response indicated and adding the total points.

Question 1 __X__ Not counted

Question 2 __X__ Not counted

Question 3 __X__ Not counted

Question 4 _____ Most of the time I lost *or* Every time I lost

Question 5 _____ Yes, most of the time *or* Yes, less than half the time I lost

Question 6 _____ Yes, in the past but not now *or* Yes

Question 7 _____ Yes

Question 8 _____ Yes

Question 9 _____ Yes

Question 10 _____ Yes

Question 11 _____ Yes

Question 12 __X__ Not counted

Question 13 _____ Yes

Question 14 _____ Yes

Question 15 _____ Yes

Question 16a _____ Yes

Question 16b _____ Yes

Question 16c _____ Yes

Question 16d _____ Yes

Question 16e _____ Yes

Question 16f _____ Yes

Question 16g _____ Yes

Question 16h _____ Yes

Question 16i _____ Yes

Question 16j __X__ Not counted
Question 16k __X__ Not counted

Total Points _____
Maximum score = 20 points
Interpreting the score:

0	No problem with gambling
1–4	Some problems with gambling
5 or more	Probable pathological gambler

Sometimes a formal clinical diagnosis, even the label "pathological gambler," can bring a person a sense of relief. You understand that you are not alone; there are other people like you. That in itself can bring hope. Jean went to see a psychiatrist because after reviewing her incomprehensible behavior around gambling, she concluded she was "crazy." Instead, the psychiatrist told her, "You're not crazy, you just need Gamblers Anonymous."

Receiving such a diagnosis finally names what's really wrong. And it's not your teenager's rebellion or the fact that you retired last year. It's gambling. The confusion, chaos, and terror you've been experiencing is the direct result of a diagnosable and treatable problem. And now that you know what it is, you can begin the journey of finding a solution.

External Clues

Sometimes the idea that you have a problem with gambling comes from someone else. It may be that a person close to you sees what's happening and confronts you with your gambling problem. Mary vividly remembers the day when her husband had found the credit card bills that she had been trying to hide. She says, "He handed me stuff about GA, and he said, 'You need help.' I knew I had pushed it just too many times."

It could be the casino personnel who take you aside and counsel you that you need to go home, or it could be trouble with the police, or family members who confront you on your behavior. Although problem gambling is much easier to hide than alcoholism or drug addiction, there are still signs that something is wrong. The Gam-Anon Web site offers the following list of clues to help families discover if they are living with a problem gambler. According to Gam-Anon, if you are living with a compulsive gambler you will answer yes to at least six of the questions.

Are You Living with a Compulsive Gambler?[10]

1. *Do you find yourself constantly bothered by bill collectors?*
2. *Is the person in question often away from home for long, unexplained periods of time?*
3. *Does this person ever lose time from work due to gambling?*
4. *Do you feel that this person cannot be trusted with money?*
5. *Does the person in question faithfully promise that he or she will stop gambling; beg, plead for another chance, yet gamble again and again?*
6. *Does this person ever gamble longer than he or she intended to, until the last dollar is gone?*
7. *Does this person immediately return to gambling to try to recover losses, or to win more?*
8. *Does this person ever gamble to get money to solve financial difficulties or have unrealistic expectations that gambling will bring the family material comfort and wealth?*
9. *Does this person borrow money to gamble with or to pay gambling debts?*
10. *Has this person's reputation ever suffered due to gambling, even to the extent of committing illegal acts to finance gambling?*

Are You Living with a Compulsive Gambler? is reprinted from the official Gam-Anon Web site, www.gam-anon.org, with permission.

11. *Have you come to the point of hiding money needed for living expenses, knowing that you and the rest of the family may go without food and clothing if you do not?*
12. *Do you search this person's clothing or go through his or her wallet when the opportunity presents itself, or otherwise check on his/her activities?*
13. *Does the person in question hide his or her money?*
14. *Have you noticed a personality change in the gambler as his or her gambling progresses?*
15. *Does the person in question consistently lie to cover up or deny his or her gambling activities?*
16. *Does this person use guilt induction as a method of shifting responsibilities for his or her gambling upon you?*
17. *Do you attempt to anticipate this person's moods, or try to control his or her life?*
18. *Does this person ever suffer from remorse or depression due to gambling, sometimes to the point of self-destruction?*
19. *Has the gambling ever brought you to the point of threatening to break up the family unit?*
20. *Do you feel that your life together is a nightmare?*

When family members confront you on your behavior, it can be a very difficult experience. It is a concrete sign that your life is out of whack. As one woman put it, "When I saw the pain in my husband's eyes, I thought to myself, it's come to this." Guilt, shame, and remorse are the predominant feelings. At the very least, it's a good time to investigate what your resources may be for changing the situation. Chapter 9 deals more specifically with family issues.

When Knowledge of Your Problem Isn't Enough

Knowledge isn't everything in the world of recovering from compulsive gambling. Knowing you have a real problem, or receiving a diagnosis that you are a problem gambler doesn't necessarily mean that you will wake up the next day and change your behavior. Lisa knew right away that she was in trouble with gambling, but still couldn't make herself stop:

> ▪▪▪ *After an eighteen-year marriage ended, I found myself alone in an apartment and scared about my path on my own. My life had seemed lonely and unsure as long as I can remember. At forty-six years old, no children, and two failed marriages, I did not have much hope. Not being able to find hope was very frightening as an outlook for my future.*
>
> *I had discovered gambling several months before my divorce. I remember feeling the first time gambling that it filled the hole in my heart. I knew right away that gambling was going to be a serious problem. I very quickly became addicted. I could go gambling anytime, spend as much time as I wanted, spend how much money I wanted, smoke cigarettes, feel safe in casinos, and totally "numb out." I knew down deep I was in trouble every time, every dollar spent, every drive there and every drive back home. I don't remember ever being in denial that I had become a compulsive gambler. I simply had to do it. The winning or losing was not the issue. I needed the rush of the slot machine, reaching a bonus round, seeing the points add up. I really was like a junkie who needed a fix. I would stay for twelve, sixteen, even twenty-four hours at a time. In about a year and a half, I lost over $50,000. I had nothing to show for that time or money. I was exhausted emotionally, physically, financially, and spiritually. I had abused myself and wanted to find help. I was very frightened.*
>
> *I found the local Gamblers Anonymous meeting and attended a Thursday night meeting in the company of my sister and close friend. I found hope and peace the moment I walked in the meeting. The most important piece for me in my journey of recovery has been my willingness to admit my addiction and my desire to stop gambling today. With the help of my fellow GA members, learning*

to ask my Higher Power for guidance, and my daily gratitude for finally having hope and peace in my heart, I now have eighteen months of gambling abstinence. ■■■

Although Lisa had full knowledge of her condition as a compulsive gambler that was experiencing serious consequences, she was not able to stop gambling until she hit bottom and found help from an outside resource, in this case, GA. Her story reinforces the idea that finding and getting help from others is a critical step on the road to recovery for most women. The next chapter tells how some of the women in the Internet survey reached a low point in their gambling behavior and made the decision to seek recovery.

CHAPTER 4

Hitting Bottom

"It became my sex, it became my lover, it became my mother."
■■■ **Gladys, age 45**

These few words from Gladys convey the powerful hold gambling can have over a person caught in the addiction. Gambling at this stage seems to fulfill many human needs: excitement, intimacy, and comfort. However, meeting these needs through compulsive gambling comes at a horrific price. In order to cope and survive, many women resort to lying, stealing, and other behaviors they would normally never contemplate. Ironically, gambling also provides the only escape from the scary and tenuous reality they create.

We don't know why some women can gamble harmlessly for several months or years and suddenly develop an addiction. We do know that for most women, the jump from social gambling to compulsive gambling is shorter than it is for men. One study found that the interval between social gambling and "intense" and "problem gambling" was significantly shorter for women; in fact, their average overall time span involved with gambling was found to be less than half as long as men's (8.5 years versus 19.7 years).[1] In the Internet survey, the average time of gambling involvement for women was about eight years. Several felt they were hooked within two to three months of their first experience. The fast development of gambling problems in women is called the "telescoping effect," and it also occurs in drug or alcohol addiction.

This chapter provides detailed accounts of how, for the survey respondents, gambling behavior spiraled from a form of recreation into chasing losses and a compulsive urge to continue gambling. It tells what this terrifying experience was like for some of the women, and what kinds of experiences made them turn the corner and quit.

"Spinning"

"Spinning" is a term used by some women to describe the sense of being completely out of control and at the total mercy of the cards they are dealt or the spins on the electronic slot machines. In other words, they no longer feel present in their lives. Mary describes it this way: "When I sat in front of that machine, there was nothing around me. I mean there was nobody. I didn't even know who was sitting next to me. I was totally enthralled." The person "Mary" was clearly absent during this period, as well as any troubles the real Mary was experiencing.

When a person is spinning, money is nothing but a means to prolong the experience of gambling. Although she was in serious debt in the real world, Gladys describes how this made no difference to her while she was in a spin. "Most of my gambling was in the grocery stores because they all have video poker machines," she says. "One day I hit three dollar progressives for a total of over $20,000, and within three days I was broke and had spent more. I mean it's just so, it's such a . . . it became my sex, it became my lover, it became my mother."

A person's body becomes irrelevant during a spin. One woman's bladder became extremely distended because she consistently ignored her body's signals telling her to get up from the machine and go to the bathroom. Many continue to gamble without sleep for two to three days at a time, living on coffee and cigarettes. The physical effects of being in a spin can include anxiety, depression, and stress-related problems such as poor sleep, ulcers, bowel problems, headaches, muscle pains, and even heart attacks. As Joni said, "Losing five hundred grand, you are going to be depressed." Several participants discussed their ability to keep on gambling in spite of what their body was telling them. Susan describes how even serious health consequences were not enough to interrupt the spin: "I had been on a gambling binge for seventy-two hours straight and went to work after that without sleeping," she says. "I went to my desk, keeled over, and had a heart attack at my desk. The day I got out of the hospital, I stopped at the grocery store and the first place I went to was the video poker machine."

The consequences that result from getting more money to keep on gambling regardless of the cost may occur to the person who is spinning, but it has little impact. While waiting in the cashier line to cash a check, a woman may fully understand that writing another check for money she doesn't have in the bank is, first of all, illegal; second, it will prevent her from paying her bills this month; and third, it will probably make it necessary for her to humiliate herself once again and ask for money from her brother. Yet, in a spin, she can almost casually dismiss this reality and resign herself to fact that if she is going to keep gambling, "this is what it takes." She may also engage in the wishful thinking that "this time I'll win and that won't happen." The reality doesn't hit until she leaves the card game or casino and walks out into the parking lot, broke and broken again. Some women have called this "the walk of shame."

Jessie rationalized embezzling money from her employer by telling herself she was only borrowing because she kept strict account of each dollar she had taken. Even the yearly audits didn't deter her, as she describes:

> ▪▪▪ Once a year, for six years, we had certified auditors come down and do a very strict three- or four-day audit and they never found it. Of course, I was scared to death this whole time, going home sick, shaking, sweating, not sleeping, waiting for them to leave, hoping they'd catch me on the one hand and hoping they wouldn't on the other. I wanted to stop but I couldn't. I was caught in this whirlpool going around and around and around. So they'd leave and I'd think—Oh God, you're so stupid you didn't even look where I'm doing this. ▪▪▪

During a spin, the pull to be "in action" is irresistible. As Jessie puts it, "There was nothing anybody could have said to me to make me stop. I mean I could have run through a brick wall to get to that casino."

Living a Double Life

If you gamble compulsively, one of the most oppressive burdens is living a double life. Lying to people who care about you is the high price you pay for appearing to be the competent attorney, housewife, teacher, mother, grandmother, and so on, while at the same time continuing to gamble. The lies and strategies used to hide the behavior have the effect of isolating you in your pain. These strategies may include:

- always being the first to get the mail so you can hide the bills and the credit card and bank statements
- keeping secret post office boxes where bills from hidden credit cards are sent
- pretending you have just been robbed
- using sick days at work to cover the times you are either in the casino or recovering from an all-nighter

Many women in this situation feel that they can't share their reality with anyone. As Jessie explains, "My kids and my boyfriend, who I lived with for ten years, did not know one single thing about the crime I was committing to gamble. I lied to everybody. I lied about the money I won, I lied about the money I lost, and I never told anybody I was stealing money. All this was a secret that was eating away inside me."

Clinicians sometimes refer to this part of the addictive process as being in denial; that is, you aren't admitting to yourself or others the kind of problems you are really having. However, living a double life is not just a psychological strategy to keep out the bad news. It can be a survival strategy for women who gamble compulsively. Here are some of the positive functions of living a double life:

1. It allows you to have a corner of sanity and normality away from the maelstrom of compulsive gambling.
2. It lets you experience that your identity, in fact, is not totally usurped by compulsive gambling, because you still have other roles in which you can function.
3. It allows you to keep your support system more or less intact, that is, you still have a job, a husband, a partner, children, and other people who care about you—as long as they don't find out.
4. It buys you time to either continue gambling or get to the point where you can ask for help.
5. It allows you to temporarily escape the deep stigma of being a *woman* who is a compulsive gambler.

Of course, all these "benefits" don't really work in the long run, because they are all contingent on keeping your gambling a secret and continuing to bear the burden of deceit.

Because some important needs are being somewhat met, it is reasonable to look at living a double life as a very expensive coping strategy, instead of the negative state of "being in denial." It is expensive because of all of their regrets about compulsive gambling, lying to loved ones was named as their top regret by the women in the Internet survey. In addition, when asked to describe the benefits of recovery, the women named the top two as improved emotional well-being (90 percent) and the relief of no longer lying (86 percent).[2] Clearly, while living a double life has its benefits as a coping strategy, for these women, in their own eyes, it was one of the most reprehensible behaviors of their gambling history—even worse than financial problems. One woman described her biggest regret as "the person I became while I was active in gambling."

When the survey respondents told their stories, many expressed shock that they actually did what they did to continue gambling. They saw themselves as women with strong values and can't reconcile their self-image with their behaviors. As Suzie says, "I knew I always had to sneak, and I said this is not fun. I hated it. You know, honesty and integrity were engraved in me. I was brought up like that. To sit here and live a lie is hard to take." Eileen says, "Some of the things I did are so beyond anything that I ever dreamed I would ever be capable of." One woman identified herself as a Christian, and as such, found "wasting my time, my money, my life" completely contrary to her religious values. Nevertheless, she kept on doing it until something happened that put her on the road to recovery.

Turning the Corner

An old saying around Twelve Step recovery groups is, "You know you are crazy when you keep on doing the same thing over and over, expecting different results." The question then becomes, What does it take to finally do something different? We all wish we had *the answer*, especially the women trying to quit, and the professionals and families trying to help them. The reality is that there are as many different answers as there are women with the problem. Each woman, it seems, has to draw her own line in the sand, the line she tells herself she will not step over. Sometimes she draws the line in an early stage of gambling when the consequences are not yet devastating, and sometimes she draws it in response to heavy negative consequences.

When asked, "More than anything, what made you stop gambling?" the most frequent reasons cited by the 136 women (who had at least six months of gambling abstinence) were in the category of feeling depressed, demoralized, or desperate. The next most frequent reasons had to do with fear of losing important relationships and wanting to reclaim them, as well as financial debt. Gamblers Anonymous calls this process "bottoming out." Many women in the survey were not able to stop until the consequences were devastating.[3]

For some, like Brenda, change came when the possibility of having to live on the street became very real and close:

■■■ *I was looking at being homeless in a couple of months if I didn't do something. I mean bag lady; shopping-cart time was just around the corner, or in my perception, that's the way it was. And that was where I wasn't willing to go. I had gone down all kinds of paths of deceptions and poverty and whatever, paths that would have been unthinkable to me a couple of years before. But being on the street, pushing a shopping cart around, and sleeping under bridges was where I wasn't willing to go—and it was coming.* ■■■

Sometimes, the line in the sand is potential suicide. There is consistent evidence that thinking about suicide, attempting suicide, and succeeding in suicide are behaviors that increase with gambling severity. For example, in one study of compulsive gambling patients attending treatment services, 30 percent had previous suicide attempts; in another study, 70 percent had experienced suicidal thoughts, and 28 percent had made actual attempts.[4] When asked what made her want to get into recovery from gambling, Joni describes this pivotal experience:

> ■■■ What happened was that I was on my way home from the casino one morning and I had lost again. I was wondering how I was going to get the money to cover the checks I had just written. I had this feeling that it would be a lot easier for me to go home, put my truck in the garage [with the engine running], shut the door, and go to sleep. Immediately after that I got to my house and I thought, you know, what a selfish act that is, and I have three kids. And my family, what they would feel if I'd done something like that. I just wasn't myself and I knew I needed help. I knew I needed professional help, because I had tried quitting on my own before many times. So I started calling different places. For hours and hours calling, starting with the Gambling Hotline. ■■■

For other women, change comes when they realize their loved ones are going to abandon them. Brenda turned the corner when her grown children told her she had used up all her promises to change, and this was her last chance. As she explains, "They were angry, and they had all kinds of reasons to be. They were tired of trying to think how to help and what to do with me. It was just overwhelming to them. I knew they loved me, but they were tired of being associated with all the problems I brought them to. They basically were saying this is your last chance, and they had given me a gazillion last chances."

For another woman, Suzie, the turnaround came after her husband said he would *not* abandon her. She had been in recovery and then relapsed, lost a lot of money, and finally told her husband about an $8,000 credit card debt she had been hiding in hopes of paying it off without him knowing. She thought "Oh, he's gonna absolutely kill me. I thought this would send him over the edge. And yet he was very understanding. He said, 'It's not the money, honey, I just want you back. You know if I have to be in a trailer house, I'll do that.' And I thought, you know, I can't take this person down with me."

Sometimes the catalyst for a woman to stop gambling is the heavy hand of the law. Julie brought this on herself after gambling away (again) all the money her husband had given her to pay bills. A way out occurred to her when she called her husband and found herself telling him she had been robbed in the grocery store parking lot. At the police station, she talked to a detective "who knew something was up." He followed her home to make sure she was safe. While talking to her husband, he asked, "Does your wife gamble?" Although her husband stated she didn't gamble anymore, the detective said he would arrest her and put her in jail if he found out the "robbery" was all about gambling. As Julie explains:

▪▪▪ *I just crawled in bed. Just let this mattress swallow me, let it just smother me to death. I wanted to die, I just couldn't figure out exactly how I wanted to do it. I was afraid of guns . . . I figured I'd wind up being an invalid, and there would be more of a burden on my family. Pills . . . what kind of pills do we have in the house? So . . . my husband came and lay down beside me, and it's probably the most gentle he's ever been. And I think because he knew I was sick and he told me what the policeman said and he said, "If you have gambled, it's OK. We'll handle it, but I need to know." So I fessed up, and the next day we called the detective. He told me he would bury the report, but he said, "I'll tell you what . . . if I ever catch you out gambling, ever, I will arrest you on the spot."* ▪▪▪

The dramatic ending to Jessie's embezzlement of company funds came when several cars drove up her driveway one morning. The company had discovered what she was doing, and officials were there to pick up all the paperwork in her home and arrest her. She was handcuffed in front of neighbors and family. Jessie said, "I think I lost the desire to gamble after that. I never even got an urge to gamble. But I still don't know if I would have quit had I not gotten caught. I probably would be dead by now."

Leslie was miserable, but until she got into serious legal trouble for embezzlement, she couldn't stop gambling. As she describes it:

> ▪▪▪ I was writing hot checks day after day after day . . . staying out until the wee hours of the morning night after night after night . . . lying to my husband, to my in-laws, to everybody . . . running to answer the phone before anybody else could, before my husband could, so he didn't hear from the bill collectors . . . grabbing the mail, making sure that he didn't see the mail, particularly bank statements. He definitely knew I was a problem gambler, but he didn't know to what extent. The final straw was getting into serious legal trouble for embezzlement. That's what finally prompted me to call GA, because I knew there was a huge possibility that I was going to go to prison. I finally had to admit that I needed help. I couldn't do it alone anymore . . . I tried that hundreds of times. ▪▪▪

Many woman are pushed to the point of "pitiful and incomprehensible demoralization," as Gamblers Anonymous describes it, before they were able to do anything different.[5] For Sheila, it took this experience, and the strong arms of the casino security, for her to finally seek help. As she describes it:

> ▪▪▪ I went into the bathroom at the casino and I just broke down completely, and one of the girls that worked the floor came in and asked me if she could help. She wanted to take me to the office, and I didn't want to go. I fought with her, so she said, "You can

either walk with me or walk with Security." I wanted to just walk to some deserted woods area and just sit there until I died without food or water. In the meantime they were guarding me there, not letting me go. My mom came and we sat there and everybody calmed me down and told me what I had to do as far as calling Gamblers Anonymous. And they called my husband and told him that they had me, and told him what he had to do as far as barring me to not allow me in the casino again. ■■■

For other women, the turning point arrived and recovery began with the tiny kindling of hope by another person: a sense that they were not alone, they were not crazy, and they could, somehow, stop gambling. Jean felt she was at a dead end when she went to her first GA meeting. "I was at a place where I had nowhere else to turn. At my first meeting the little voice in my head kept saying 'Who do you think you're trying to kid? . . . You can't quit, there's no way you can quit.' And then someone in the meeting told me I could quit. I didn't quit right away, but I started thinking that way."

The stories of these women point to one truth. There is no one tried and true path to choosing recovery. Each woman's line in the sand is unique, just as each woman herself is. It is also clear that these women tended to look more and more alike the closer they got to their "bottom." They all became accomplished actresses in their ability to lead a double life; they all lied, felt incredible shame, tried over and over to quit gambling, endured physical duress and stress, threatened the well-being of family and loved ones, thought about suicide, moved closer to financial ruin every day, and blew past many self-prescribed limits they never imagined they would ignore. Ultimately, these women found the particular line in the sand they would not cross and began their journey into recovery. However, they did not take their lives back from compulsive gambling without a real fight.

The second part of this book, "Finding Your Way Out: Recovery Options," details the steps taken by the women who succeeded in stopping gambling. In chapters 5 through 9 we'll explore their good and bad experiences with Gamblers Anonymous, their use of professional help, and the stories of those who stopped "on their own." We'll also see how their families both helped them and hindered them, and in chapter 10 we'll focus on the challenges and methods of maintaining recovery.

PART 2: Finding Your Way Out: Recovery Options

CHAPTER 5

Relapse and the Recovery Process: "The Long and Winding Road . . ."

"You're coming to meetings, you're going away, and you're hanging on by your fingernails." ■■■ **Jessie, age 54**

If you are at all familiar with the Beatles, you probably sang the subtitle of the chapter in your head as you read it. Who can forget this plaintive ballad, first recorded in 1970? Parts of the song could serve as the compulsive gamblers' lament, particularly the lines about being left with a "pool of tears" and not knowing which way to turn.

Without stretching this analogy too far, the second part of this book is about finding your way. The overall purpose is to suggest a toolbox of recovery options that are based on the real-life experience of the recovering women who responded to the Internet survey. The respondents have the shared experience of being women in this culture, which impacts the context of their addiction and recovery. However, their personal experiences reveal very different goals, different methods for achieving goals, and different measurements of success. The following chapters describe the bumps along the road to stopping gambling, and the women's mix of positive and negative experiences with professional help, with Gamblers Anonymous, with family support, and with getting well "on their own." The struggles and triumphs of maintaining recovery are discussed in the last chapter.

Relapse and Recovery

Today, most professionals in addiction treatment recognize that relapse is a part of the recovery process. This understanding can be partly attributed to the widespread acceptance of a six-stage change process discerned and developed by James Prochaska and Carlo DiClemente in 1986.[1] According to their research, everyone goes through a similar change process, whether a person is trying to stop smoking or change a habit such as lateness. One of the stages of this change model is a setback of some kind, or a relapse.

Think of the stages of change model as a circle like a pie, and each stage is a piece of that pie. The stages are listed here, including how each might look in the process of entering recovery from compulsive gambling:

1. Precontemplation: You don't even think you have a gambling problem, even though others do.
2. Contemplation: You think that maybe you have a problem; maybe you're too far in debt; maybe your brother has a small point; you can see the advantages of stopping gambling but you don't want to give it up.
3. Preparation: You wonder what you did with the hotline number you'd been carrying around for months. What's Gamblers Anonymous?
4. Action: You decide you'll go to the treatment group three times a week; you'll hand over your checkbook to your sister.
5. Maintenance: You go to GA meetings on Mondays and Thursdays; you take up skydiving and/or bridge.

6. Relapse: You weren't even thinking about gambling, but then you heard an ad for the casino on the radio, and before you knew it, your car pointed that direction.

In other words, change is a complex process, and it's normal for people to go around the pie circle through the stages many times before a change is solidly in place. The most difficult stage is the maintenance stage—hanging on to the change. This will be the topic of chapter 10. Ever tried to lose weight and keep it off?

Sometimes, relapse can be looked at as a positive experience (in hindsight), because it gives you a better sense of how strong your problem really is and how hard you have to work to overcome it. Many women, like Alice, start out with the notion that their gambling habit is not so bad (not as bad as some people's!). It took a relapse for her to open her eyes to reality. Here is Alice's story:

▪▪▪ *Teaching was the one constant in my life. Up and down, around and about, no matter what happened, I always had a way of supporting my two children and myself. I have been and will always be forever thankful that I had thirty-three challenging, fun-filled, productive years in education. However, upon retirement, I found myself faced with the dilemma of what do I do now? I tried volunteering, cooking, gardening, reading, and so on, but nothing quite satisfied nor completed me the way my career had. That is, until I rediscovered the casino. You see, friends and I had tasted the bittersweet gambling scene occasionally in the years prior to my retirement. Nothing serious, really, just a fun little afternoon adventure.*

However, with time on my hands and money to spare, gambling soon became routine. I'd awake in the morning, get my chores for the day taken care of and head out to the casino "Where The Fun Never Ends!" I rarely won anything. It wasn't necessary. Winning money was a secondary benefit. I was there to escape. Escape boredom, responsibility, life, problems, people, and obligations. And guess what? It worked! I had a new reason to live! This was the most fun I had ever had, and the most destructive. Once in a while a little angel would tap me on the shoulder and ask, "What in the heck are you doing?" Denial is a very powerful defense mechanism. I didn't have a problem. I never smoked, drank much, nor did drugs. I had great parents, raised terrific kids, and paid my bills on time. This couldn't be happening to me! For God's sake, I'm a Catholic! Well, guess what? When it came to addiction, none of that mattered.

Neither did any of the deals I made with myself, such as leave when I double my money, leave when I hit a jackpot, leave when my cash was gone, leave after four hours. Leave, leave, leave. What a joke. I couldn't and didn't leave. Oh, did I tell you that I had turned into a liar? "I'll be home in a couple of hours, honey." " I think I'll go shopping." "My sister and I are going for a ride." Liar, liar, liar.

This kind of escalating behavior did not help my self-esteem. I felt ridiculously stupid and remorsefully demoralized. I needed help and I found it at a Gamblers Anonymous meeting. Not that I wanted to be there. I hated it and everyone in the room. After attending for three months, I decided that I had made a mistake. I wasn't like all those other gamblers in the room. I actually could gamble, and I ventured forth to prove my new assertion. Only things didn't work out as planned. I quickly ended up on my face, scared senseless and humbled. That's when the miracles began to happen!

I started to listen at meetings and in so doing began to relate to my fellow gamblers. I began to feel an intangible spirituality available there. Something happened during those meetings that lifted the pressure and gave me hope that I might be able to arrest this constant need to self-destruct. That relief was there for the taking and open to anyone regardless of any religious preference. The room was filled with believers and nonbelievers and everything in between. The spirituality I found was available to all and free for the taking. I found a genuine love that was bigger and broader than I had ever imagined, available to anyone who would try. I prayed often, went to meetings, and worked the Steps.

I began to get a glimpse of understanding that my addiction was not "my fault," it was just the way it was. I found I no longer had to worry about whose "fault" anything is. I used to point the finger at everyone else when something went wrong in my life. Someone in GA asked me one time, "What is your part in it?" What do you mean? I asked. Then it dawned on me that I do have a part in every single thing I want to blame on someone else. When I look honestly at my part, I no longer get on my high horse.

I also learned I don't have all the answers to other people's problems. I learned to shut up around my grown daughter and stop pushing my agenda onto her. I stopped being so critical of her behavior and started seeing her good points for a change. As a result, our relationship has gotten much better and we actually can enjoy each other's company.

Now that I have nearly five years of gamble-free living, days will go by when I don't even think about gambling. When I do, it's not nearly the problem it was because I have some distance from it. Distance has given me the gift of being able to think it through and not automatically react to an urge to gamble. I still go to meetings once or twice a week because it helps me to stay spiritually fit, and it helps to check my compulsions. To this day I still am learning, praying, and trying to be a better person today than I was yesterday. ▪▪▪

Alice's relapse was pivotal to beginning her long-term recovery. Many books about addiction start with the problem, then move on to recovery, and then take up relapse. In this book, we start looking at the recovery process by examining relapse *first*, because it's helpful (and hopeful) with compulsive gambling to view relapse as the beginning of that process. The intent here is to offer hope—grounded in the experience of these recovering women—that no matter how many times you go back to gambling after making a firm decision never to do it again, change can still happen. For the compulsive gambler, quitting is usually not a straight shot: realizing the need to stop and then just stopping. Although some women do stop gambling after they understand what a problem it has become, often the process takes a circuitous route that begins when a person first *tries* to stop. Even if you don't succeed at first, trying is the first step that may need to be taken over and over again until you do stop.

"Recovery Ain't for Sissies"

In order to look squarely at the phenomenon of relapse, it's important to notice what kinds of conditions a woman is likely to find herself in once she decides to quit gambling. Stepping through the door to recovery can be a little like stepping into some special version of hell, at least initially. Some of the reasons are discussed here in this chapter—not to undermine hope or provide excuses for relapse, but to show that in spite of all these potential problems, women can and do stop gambling.

Just like alcoholics and drug addicts, many gamblers experience withdrawal symptoms when they stop gambling. One study found that 65 percent of compulsive gamblers reported at least one physical side effect upon quitting, symptoms such as sleeplessness, headaches, loss of appetite, physical weakness, heart racing, muscle aches, breathing difficulties, and chills.[2] This may last for a few weeks or longer. At the same time, the brain of the compulsive gambler is likely to be out of whack, as we noted in chapter 2. This makes it difficult to focus, make decisions, and control emotions—all at a time when you need these skills to stop gambling. Withdrawal effects listed by the women in the Internet survey include:

- laziness
- weakened leg muscles
- weight gain
- the sense of losing a best friend or security blanket
- trouble finding any activity to fill the loneliness and boredom the way gambling did
- depression
- anxieties and fear about ability to follow through
- increase in other addictive behaviors
- irritability and lack of patience with children
- feelings ranging from guilt, depression, and mood swings to a total loss of self-understanding
- extreme boredom, nervousness
- missing gambling acquaintances, camaraderie, and easygoing banter
- old debts finally catching up
- extreme night sweats, rapid heart rate, anxiety, and a general ill-at-ease feeling

Withdrawal symptoms may be easier to bear than the crushing burden of financial debt that a woman has to face when she stops gambling. Many don't even know the reality of their financial status because they can't bear to look. By the time they stopped, the 136 women in the Internet survey had an average gambling debt of $46,670. Nearly two-thirds of them (63 percent) reported losing $1,000 or more in one night. The Ontario study found that on average, the women surveyed spent the equivalent of 80 percent of their salary on gambling.[3]

For most gamblers, there is no quick fix to the financial crisis they find themselves in when they quit. For women, fixing the finances is likely to be even slower than for men because they don't have equal earning power. According to a 2004 Government Accounting Office report, working women's wages still lag behind men's, averaging eighty cents on the dollar. This figure holds true regardless of occupation, education, industry, race, marital status, and job tenure.[4]

Brenda, one of the survey respondents, has seen "many, many" women in recovery who still "don't know if they are going to be able to pay the electricity bill." As she sees it, "Whatever else it does to you, it devastates you financially. And it takes awhile, especially the kind of jobs that women are usually in. It's not like we can put together a presentation and go land some dynamite job that's going to make a couple hundred thousand dollars pour in." The prospect of a bleak future—barely making ends meet for months, years, even the rest of your life—makes it hard to focus on stopping gambling. This is especially true because the addicted brain tells you that a huge gambling win may be the *only* way to recoup your losses. Such a notion is reinforced by memories of winning jackpots, the awareness of other people's wins, and the enticements and promotions of the gambling industry. Some of the women in the Internet survey said that dealing with financial stress was the hardest part of their recovery. In the words of four of them:

- "Paying off the damn bills!"
- "Getting creditors to help you out."
- "Never being free of financial struggles."
- "Getting my debts paid off."

In spite of the financial burden, these women were able to cope and remain gambling free. For them, living life without the tyranny of compulsive gambling was worth it. When asked what was the most satisfying part of their recovery, these same four women had this to say:

- ▪ "Knowing that I'm not alone."
- ▪ "Establishing a payment plan with creditors."
- ▪ "Freedom to spend time in other ways. No more lying about what I'm doing or feeling."
- ▪ "Life can be stressful sometimes, but I can now deal with the stress by going to GA and not to the casinos."

Jessie faced an insurmountable debt to repay because of embezzling from her employer for gambling money. One may wonder how a person who has gone to prison for her crime can get out and then face this overwhelming responsibility. Here's how she reframed her financial burden into something she could do, would do, and felt good about doing:

> ▪▪▪ *I will be paying back my victim for another 175 years. They know I can never pay it back, and I know I can never pay it back. But I do make my payments and I think it is to remind me that I committed a crime and I will be paying for it. But that's OK. I know there were two things wrong when I went to prison. One was that I was a compulsive gambler, which was taken care of, and the other one was that I committed a crime, which I was sentenced to and I served my time. So I feel like I am taking care of both of them and I will be working on my recovery for the rest of my life, besides paying back my victim, so that is fine.*
>
> *I'm working now. I am seventy years old and I will work for another year to save up enough money to retire on. Hopefully, I'll be able to retire and pay the necessary bills I have, which is just the modest rent and lights and all that stuff. But if I get that, and can still work for people in Gamblers Anonymous, I'm fine. I'll never*

have what I had, and maybe I should thank God for that, because
the things I had weren't very healthy. ■ ■ ■

In this example, Jessie's actions seem to embody the spirit of the Serenity Prayer—"the serenity to accept the things I cannot change, the courage to change the things I can." Her wisdom is not only "knowing the difference," but also knowing how to approach such a momentous task on a daily basis.

Family support, or lack of it, is a critical issue when you stop gambling. Suffice it to say that there is something about a woman gambling away all the household money or borrowing and not paying back money from close relatives that tends to drive them away. Just as in the alcoholism arena, husbands of women with gambling problems are more likely to leave the marriage than wives of men with gambling problems. In the Canadian study on women with gambling problems, Boughton found that support systems for women who wanted to change their behavior were very limited; 18 percent felt they had no support at all.[5] When asked, "What was the most important support system in your recovery?" 70 percent of the women in the Internet survey put Gamblers Anonymous at the top of the list, 36 percent reported a spouse or partner as most supportive, and 18 percent reported parents. Compulsive gambling is a lonely problem. Even if you still have your friends and family around, you are likely to be isolated from them emotionally. They don't know all of what you've done to maintain your gambling addiction, and they don't understand the part they do know about.

Finally, getting help of any kind may be a problem unless you live in or near a mid-size to large city in a state that funds gambling treatment. Oregon and Indiana, for example, have comprehensive treatment programs with a good deal of accessibility throughout the state. Unfortunately, many areas are short on readily available treatment options. You may have to travel some distance to find a GA meeting, or you may find yourself going to a substance abuse counselor who knows nothing about gambling addiction. The good news is that more states are stepping up to fund gambling treatment; more training is being offered to professional counselors; the Internet provides blogs, chat rooms, and informational resources, and GA offers help at no cost.

Modern women, including those who become compulsive gamblers, are expected to play a variety of roles, such as mother, employee, partner or spouse, caretaker of friends and immediate family, and in an old-fashioned sense, keeper of the hearth. For women, one key reason to quit gambling is the fear that they may lose their connections to family and friends, and in some cases, lose custody of their children. When a woman stops gambling, she may throw herself back into the roles she feels she has neglected, trying to reconnect emotionally. An anonymous therapist who works full-time with male and female problem gamblers describes how the differences in their daily lives may affect their efforts to quit:

■■■ *When I explore what the material concerns are in their [women's] daily lives, I often discover that they are working, taking care of practically every household detail, dealing with children and in-laws and, additionally, dealing with ghosts of the past. Invariably, male clients do not deal with all of these issues; they just gamble and work. It seems so easy for the men that I wonder how all of them can't suddenly experience full recovery in a hurry. And many do, as a matter of fact. But the women: they have so damn much to do in a day that even the all-consuming nature of problem gambling does not allow them to avoid.*[6] ■■■

With all of these potential problems, it's easy to understand that just like old age, "Recovery ain't for sissies." Fortunately, there are many benefits to stopping gambling that can carry a person through to the other side where life starts to look good again. But in the process of abstaining for any length of time, most gamblers have to deal with relapses.

Relapses and Lapses

No one likes to deal with relapse. It can be perceived as evidence of a failure in many different arenas; for example, as a treatment setback, as evidence of not "working the GA program" well enough, as yet another betrayal of family and friends, and, for the gambler, as another confirmation of her "no-goodness." Suzie describes this feeling as "dying inside." She says, "You know you're not supposed to be there and that I'm letting down this person, that person in recovery, my husband, or my in-laws or whoever believed in me. I'd be taking in that guilt and the weight of the guilt is tremendous. It was like 'My God, you're sick, I mean, here you are, you got everything going for you and you're blowing it, big time.'"

Yet multiple relapses are a common occurrence before a person can actually stop gambling. In one recent study, 92 percent of the participants who qualified as compulsive gamblers and had a goal of abstinence relapsed at least once during one year. Other studies of gamblers who entered treatment programs show similar high rates of relapse, from 71 to 85 percent.[7] Although there is no clear definition of the difference, "lapse" is generally understood to be a short, temporary return to gambling, and "relapse" signals that the person has gone back to uncontrolled gambling that has many negative consequences. Both types are common to the recovery process of drug and alcohol addictions, not just gambling.

The difficult conditions that exist when a woman stops gambling—withdrawal, estranged family and friends, financial problems—are commonly experienced by any addict who is giving up an addictive substance or behavior. Since practicing the addiction has become the primary coping tool for any problems that come up in life, even ordinary problems can look insurmountable. The biggest problem for Joanne, in her words, was "LIFE!" She says, "You have to learn how to deal with what is going on. I had to start dealing with everything, which is very difficult. I had to stop hiding."

But the compulsive gambler has one unique difficulty that contributes to relapse. Gambling is the only addiction that offers both escape *and* the possibility of financial rewards for engaging in the behavior. The compulsive gambler's brain has been conditioned over and over by an intermittent reward schedule, telling the gambler, "You're due for a win." That optimism about winning can send gamblers right to the casino or card room to make up their losses and have something to offer their creditors.

Many treatment professionals believe that a gambler does plan a relapse on some level of consciousness, but to the gambler it can seem to "come out of the blue." Sarah had not gambled for one year and was going to therapy three times a week, and "then, I don't know, it's just that one day I was at the 7-Eleven, and I just threw a couple of quarters in while I was waiting to be checked out and that was it. . . . I started gambling heavily, doing crazy things like writing bad checks, and lost my job."

Although a relapse may feel completely impulsive, recent research has shed some light on the reasons and conditions in which compulsive gamblers relapse. Relapse was found to occur most frequently in the evenings when a person was alone and thinking about finances (70 percent), alone and frustrated (53 percent), or alone and happy (49 percent). The most frequently reported reason for relapse was optimism about winning (reported for 24 percent of the male relapses, 21 percent of the female). Other reasons in the top categories have significant differences between men and women. Men were more likely to report feeling financial pressures to make money or chase losses (22 percent, versus 7 percent for women); and women were more likely to report dealing with negative emotions as the main reason (18 percent, versus 7 percent for men).[8] As Sarah reports, "You can slip with your addiction and you can slip with your recovery because your life becomes so overwhelming that you automatically go back into your addiction. It is the only thing that eases the pain."

"Dealing with negative emotions or situations" is one of the major reasons women relapse, according to the research cited above. The types of emotions include anger, frustration, anxiety, loneliness, and guilt; situations include feeling the "need to get away from" problems with children, work difficulties, and so on. After handing her money and credit cards over to her fiancé to manage so she wouldn't gamble, Jane began to resent the arrangement. She recalls thinking, "This is so unfair that I don't get to handle my own money, and I'm not even married to this person. Why should I let him have everything that I make?" She says, "I would really talk myself into a frenzy about how I was like 'poor me, poor me.' I took the credit card and I went out and stayed all night in the casino gambling so that I could really make a statement to him about how much I didn't want him to control me. I said I wanted to be free, but what was going on in my brain was that I just wanted to be free to go gamble."

In the research study cited on page 70, unstructured time or boredom was a reason for relapsing in 17 percent of the men and 7 percent of the women.[9] But in the Internet survey, "feeling bored" was actually the top reason for gambling reported, followed by "feeling lonely," "looking for fun," and "depressed about their life or future ." As one retired woman put it, "I didn't know what to do with myself when I quit gambling. That's all I'd done to fill the time for so long, ever since my retirement. I had to put together a life that was completely foreign to me, and one that didn't cost any money. Nothing interested me, except going back to gambling."

Australian women also reported boredom, loneliness, and stress as the motivation for gambling in a study by Sarah Brown and Louise Coventry. The authors suggested that because our modern social structure is based upon competition, order, and merit, gambling provides a brief opportunity to enter a "play-world" where the differences in people's skills, abilities, and resources temporarily disappear.[10] Going back to gambling may also offer temporary relief from the overburdened routine and constant demand to tend relationships that many women experience day after day.

It's important to keep in mind that although the women in the Internet survey experienced relapses, slightly more than one-third were able to stop gambling in a relatively short time (four and a half months) once they knew in their hearts they needed to stop. All 136 had stopped gambling for at least six months at the time of the survey, and the average length of abstinence was about three years. How did they get past the siren call to gamble again, in spite of all the difficult circumstances noted above? Their many different paths to recovery will be explored in the next four chapters. Practical tips on what to do if a relapse occurs are found in chapter 10.

CHAPTER 6

Gamblers Anonymous and Gam-Anon

"It was like a bucket of cold water was dumped on my head. But I think what it was, was reading those Twenty Questions. I went, 'Ahhh, ahhh, yes, yes, yeeesss.'" ▪▪▪ **Irene, age 36**

Answering the Gamblers Anonymous Twenty Questions for yourself (see pages 31–32) can be a real eye-opener, as Irene points out. In typical GA meetings, someone reads these questions as part of the opening of the meeting, and members respond out loud. Thankfully, no matter how many questions you answer yes, you find out you are not alone. Thousands have shared the same kind of misery about their gambling, and managed to stop gambling in spite of these behaviors. Some of those people are right there in the same room with you to offer help and support.

Because more and more women are attending GA, the meetings themselves are becoming more in tune with women's experiences. However, even up until a few years ago, men (who didn't always understand what to do with women) primarily dominated GA. According to the Arizona Council on Compulsive Gambling Web site, even though GA started in that state in 1973, few women attended meetings.

■ ■ ■ *For the first 18 years, a few women walked through the doors . . . and left. By their own admission, the men didn't quite know what to do with them. The women were told they hadn't gambled long enough; they hadn't lost enough to be real gamblers. . . . They didn't play real games. . . . Their tears and their stories were ridiculed. They were "hit on," "let's go for coffee . . . at my place, baby . . ." They didn't stay. The men said, "Women just don't seem to have what it takes to stay in recovery."[1]* ■ ■ ■

The recent influx of women into the program has helped men understand the seriousness of women's gambling problems and that women do have what it takes to stay in recovery. Nationwide estimates of women's attendance at Gamblers Anonymous meetings range from 33 to 50 percent of attendees, a dramatic increase from the early 1980s when gambling treatment pioneer Robert Custer estimated it at 4 percent.[2] Some of these pioneering women made it easier for the rest of us, by persisting when faced with disbelief and misunderstanding. Jean was a bingo gambler, and when she finally got to GA in 1993 she found that many of the members, mostly men, did not understand how this could be a problem. She got through this misunderstanding by just ignoring them. She says, "Nobody had to tell me whether I had a problem or not. I wanted help so bad, I didn't care what they thought."

The majority (75 percent) of the women in the Internet study had attended at least one meeting of GA.[3] Their experience with this organization was almost entirely positive. Many claimed it "saved my life," yet for a few, it did not help at all. There were some initial challenges for many women who attended the meetings. Some had never attended a Twelve Step mutual-help meeting of any kind, and balked at the mere suggestion that they might need or receive help from an organization such as GA. Others who had been sober many years through regular attendance at Alcoholics Anonymous initially complained that the GA members were not running their meetings correctly (the AA way).

Whether you are brand new to these programs or a seasoned Twelve Step member, it may help to take a look at what the GA program offers and how it builds on, but is different from, other Twelve Step programs.

What Is Gamblers Anonymous?

Gamblers Anonymous is a Twelve Step mutual-help program of men and women "who share their experience, strength and hope with each other that they may solve their common problem and help others to recover from a gambling problem."[4] The GA program acknowledges Alcoholics Anonymous (AA) as a guide and foundation, and utilizes steps of recovery and organizational principles very similar to those of AA. One of the basic principles is the anonymity of the members, as described in Step Twelve of the Unity Program (see page 78).

The Unity Program of Gamblers Anonymous[5]

In order to maintain unity our experience has shown that:

1. *Our common welfare should come first; personal recovery depends upon group unity.*
2. *Our leaders are but trusted servants; they do not govern.*
3. *The only requirement for Gamblers Anonymous membership is a desire to stop gambling.*
4. *Each group should be self-governing except in matters affecting other groups or Gamblers Anonymous as a whole.*
5. *Gamblers Anonymous has but one primary purpose—to carry its message to the compulsive gambler who still suffers.*
6. *Gamblers Anonymous ought never endorse, finance or lend the Gamblers Anonymous name to any related facility or outside*

> enterprise, lest problems of money, property and prestige divert us from our primary purpose.
>
> 7. Every Gamblers Anonymous Group ought to be fully self-supporting, declining outside contributions.
>
> 8. Gamblers Anonymous should remain forever non-professional, but our service centers may employ special workers.
>
> 9. Gamblers Anonymous, as such, ought never be organized; but we may create service boards or committees directly responsible to those they serve.
>
> 10. Gamblers Anonymous has no opinion on outside issues; hence the Gamblers Anonymous name ought never be drawn into public controversy.
>
> 11. Our public relations policy is based on attraction rather than promotion; we need always maintain personal anonymity at the level of press, radio, films and television.
>
> 12. Anonymity is the spiritual foundation of the Gamblers Anonymous program, ever reminding us to place principles before personalities.

As is customary in Twelve Step groups, the final "diagnosis" of whether a person is a compulsive gambler is left up to the person. The only requirement for membership is "a desire to stop gambling."[6] GA does not prescribe abstinence; rather, the organization was developed to help individuals who *have abstinence from gambling as a goal*. GA is not for people who want to cut down or moderate their gambling; it is for people who have already tried various strategies of moderation and found they couldn't stick to their resolutions. As one woman described it (using as a model a well-read section of *Alcoholics Anonymous*, also known as the "Big Book"), "I tried everything . . . leaving my credit cards at home, not carrying around my checkbook, scheduling gambling for only a short period when I knew I had to leave, setting *abso-*

lute limits on the amount of money I would spend, banning my-self from the casino, going to church, reading uplifting literature, taking vitamins, taking antidepressants, learning how to knit . . . Nothing worked!" Therefore, no matter how bitter the abstinence pill appeared to be, they have understood for themselves that the only way for them to have a normal life is to quit gambling al-together. GA is there to help them do it.

Recovering gamblers, not addiction professionals, run the GA program; meetings take place in various hospitable places around town (senior centers, church basements, and so on). The meetings may be run a little differently from group to group. Some groups are very structured (start and end on time, no crosstalk or giving advice) and others take a more relaxed approach to the guidelines. It's a good idea to visit more than one meeting, if possible, to find one that best meets your needs. Some GA meetings recom-mend that the newcomer attend ninety meetings in ninety days, just as in Alcoholics Anonymous. However, it may be impossible to attend that many consecutive meetings, as GA groups don't meet that often in most communities. The GA pamphlet known as the "Combo Book" stresses that "meetings make it," and rec-ommends that newcomers attend "as many meetings as possible, but at least one full meeting per week."[7]

Like AA, GA is fundamentally a spiritual program, and elimi-nating gambling is only the beginning of the recovery process. The majority of the Twelve Steps of GA involve addressing "char-acter defects" such as "lying, stealing, avoiding reality and escap-ing into a dream world, or sometimes indulging in all three," and building a life based on spiritual principles (see page 82).[8] It is not a Christian organization, nor is it affiliated with any particular religion. The GA writings about spiritual growth typically refer to "God, *as I understand him*." Although some GA meetings in the United States close with a Christian prayer, many groups stick to the nondenominational Serenity Prayer ("God, grant me the serenity to accept the things I cannot change, the courage to change the things I can, and the wisdom to know the difference").

Some of the many strengths of Gamblers Anonymous include:

- It is accessible in all fifty states and online (www.gamblers anonymous.org), and may be the only resource available in more rural areas to address compulsive gambling.

- The price is right (no dues or fees), especially for compulsive gamblers who are likely to have crippling debt and financial difficulties. GA supports itself (pays rent, buys literature) from voluntary member contributions. You are asked not to contribute at your first meeting.

- It can provide extremely valuable social support for people who have alienated their families and friends and are likely to feel very alone.

- The GA Twenty Questions (see pages 31–32) that helps people decide if they are compulsive gamblers is largely comparable to other professionally developed criteria.

- GA offers acceptance by people who uniquely understand all the degradations involved in practicing compulsive gambling. It is run entirely by recovering compulsive gamblers who have done the things most gamblers do to support their addiction, and who now volunteer their time to be sponsors, chair meetings, arrange for meeting places, secure GA literature, and respond to requests for help day and night.

- Research studies have suggested that when GA is combined with professional treatment or therapy, there are positive results.[9]

- At the first meeting, newcomers can listen to other people's stories of how they got to GA and how they used the Twelve Steps to stop gambling. Newcomers are usually offered (free) pamphlets about gambling and the GA program, and phone numbers of people who want to help. Sponsors are available to give more ongoing and personal support in quitting gambling and working through the Steps.

- Family members and friends are welcome at "open" meetings.

Gamblers Anonymous is not without its critics. Like other Twelve Step programs, it is criticized for its sole focus on gambling to the exclusion of other co-existing addictions and mental health issues such as depression and anxiety. Other criticisms include:

- There is a lack of evidence in formal research studies that attending GA alone is effective in achieving abstinence.[10]

- GA may focus more on financial problems than spiritual growth. For example, the "pressure relief group," made up of GA members who have been successful in stopping gambling, is a special group that meets outside of the regular GA meeting to help newcomers address their finances and their spouses or family members. This practical aspect of GA is different from the workings of Twelve Step groups focusing on substance abuse. The rewording of the Twelve Steps from the original AA version also reflects a more secular focus. For example, GA's Step Twelve says to make "an effort to practice these principles in all our affairs," without mentioning the "spiritual awakening" of the AA version. GA's Step Three refers to the "Power of our own understanding," while AA's refers to "God of our understanding."

- Historically, GA has not been inviting to women or others whose needs may differ from those of the dominant middle-class male, although this is rapidly changing. Like the AA Big Book, GA's literature was written primarily using the male pronouns "he" and "him," and this has not changed. Yet.

The Twelve Steps of Gamblers Anonymous

1. *We admitted we were powerless over gambling—that our lives had become unmanageable.*

2. *Came to believe that a Power greater than ourselves could restore us to a normal way of thinking and living.*

3. *Made a decision to turn our will and our lives over to the care of this Power of our own understanding.*

4. *Made a searching and fearless moral and financial inventory of ourselves.*

5. *Admitted to ourselves and to another human being the exact nature of our wrongs.*

6. *Were entirely ready to have these defects of character removed.*

7. *Humbly asked God (of our understanding) to remove our shortcomings.*

8. *Made a list of all persons we had harmed and became willing to make amends to them all.*

9. *Make direct amends to such people wherever possible, except when to do so would injure them or others.*

10. *Continued to take personal inventory and when we were wrong, promptly admitted it.*

11. *Sought through prayer and meditation to improve our conscious contact with God as we understood Him, praying only for knowledge of His will for us and the power to carry that out.*

12. *Having made an effort to practice these principles in all our affairs, we tried to carry this message to other compulsive gamblers.*

Finding a GA Meeting—and Actually Getting There

The GA Web site, www.gamblersanonymous.org, has a state-by-state directory of meetings listed by day of the week. It may also mention the type: an "open meeting" means family and friends of gamblers are welcome, a "closed meeting" is for gamblers only, and some meetings are designated "women preferred" or "men preferred." It's good to double-check the time and place: local GA members update the site with such changes, and sometimes there's a lag. To verify the details, call the 800 "Helpline" phone number available in most states. Find that number by visiting the National Council on Problem Gambling Web site at www.ncpgambling.org. (Click on the "Problem Gamblers" link, then "Help by State." Other state resources are also listed here, as well as a short screening test for problem gamblers.) State Helplines are also listed under "Gambling" in the Yellow Pages; in larger cities, the local GA may have its own listing. In casinos, flyers with the state Helpline number are often found near the cashier.

The women in the Internet survey found their way to GA through a variety of methods. About a third—37 percent—learned about it by calling a state Helpline. Professional counselors were the next most frequent referral source, followed by the Yellow Pages, a friend in GA, a physician, a family member in GA, a co-worker, and a clergyperson or pastor.[11]

But having information about GA and where to find it doesn't necessarily mean it is a straight shot to attending meetings. As Brenda explains it:

■■■ *I had never heard of Gamblers Anonymous, but I figured there is an Alcoholics Anonymous, so there has to be something like it for gamblers. So I looked it up in the phone book and sure enough there was a number. I wrote the number down and carried it around with me for a few months, thinking, well, I've done something. I didn't dial the number, but I carried it around. And then when things got so bad, I dialed. And thank God, at my first meeting there was a woman who was at her second meeting. She knew that the Twelve Steps were the answer, and she just latched on to me and didn't let go.* ■■■

Susan had to come to terms with her concerns about anonymity before she could start attending GA. Although the program stresses anonymity, and at every meeting people are encouraged to follow the policy, "Who you see here, what's said here, stays here," there is the possibility that a person could violate this rule. Susan says that for her, "The hardest thing was being humble enough to be able to talk about my gambling, because I was visible in the community. You're always concerned about anonymity, and I think it scares a lot of us. I have a degree, I have a job, and it's very hard to get to the level that you say, 'You know what, I'm sick.'" After deciding that well-educated working people also deserve a chance to get well, she felt able to attend GA.

Early Participation in GA

The slogan "Meetings make it!" is noted in the GA Combo Book and stated at the beginning of almost every GA meeting. The women in the survey who used the GA program took this advice seriously. Most of them attended meetings frequently in the early months of stopping gambling. In the first six months of their recovery, over half of the GA attendees (62 percent) reported going to two or more meetings a week, and 32 percent reported once a week.[12]

Going to your first GA meeting can be an overwhelming experience, especially if you're not familiar with Twelve Step groups.

Irene's counselor wanted her to try GA at least five times. Her response was, "Anything anonymous, *excuse me!*" Here's how she describes her first meeting:

> ▪▪▪ *I was so scared. The first meeting you sit there and you get your little packet and you're like, "Shit, what am I doing here!" And you're like, "No way." I mean I had never heard of the Twelve Steps. You know, it was a real eye-opener for me. I couldn't even really talk that first meeting, I was so choked up, I was so sick. It was like a bucket of cold water was dumped on my head. But I think what it was, was reading those Twenty Questions. I went, "Ahhh ahhh, yes, yes, yeeesss."* ▪▪▪

How were the women received when they started going to GA? In the most common response to the question "How did you feel welcomed?" 37 percent of the women said they felt understood by people with the same problem. Mary said, "I felt they understood my problem and pain." For Susan, "I felt welcomed, as all of us were suffering many of the same results of our gambling." Lisa made the point that the people at the meeting understood her, whereas her family and friends did not. An almost equal number of responses (36 percent) cited the friendly behaviors and personal attention they received.

Feelings of "belonging" and no longer feeling so alone made up 10 percent of the responses. For example, Julie stated, "By listening to everyone share their story and knowing I wasn't alone." Joanne found her sense of belonging by being asked to do service work. After a relapse, she went back to GA and after only a few weeks, the members decided she should be secretary of the meeting. Secretaries are appointed from the membership to open meetings; they make sure all the literature is available, ensure coffee is made, and generally see that everything is ready for the meeting. Consequently, Joanne didn't miss a meeting for an entire year.

Other respondents noted that meetings were the only place they could tell the truth about what had actually happened ("It was one of the first times that you didn't have to lie about everything . . . felt very good to get everything out in the open"). Perhaps most importantly, meetings instilled the hope that what seemed like in-surmountable problems could in fact be solved ("I never stopped going to meetings and somehow I knew GA was where salvation lay for me, and no matter how messed up I was, as far as relaps-ing stuff, I knew that GA was what would save me from myself"). Two participants reported that they were the only women in their meetings, but they still felt very welcome ("When I went to my first meeting, I was the only woman there. And the guys just welcomed me with open arms").

Fewer women (27 percent) listed ways they felt unwelcome when they attended GA.[13] Many of these responses involved feel-ing unwelcome as a woman, for example, "The men didn't think slot players were real gamblers," "I'm a woman, so they ignored me the first three months," and "'Good old boys' in charge (not too many women there)." One woman explained, "I went to GA and they did not discuss gambling—they discussed sports. I was the only woman and stopped going. I felt like I was attending a lonely hearts club with men."

Other negative reactions involved problems with how the GA program was being practiced. One woman noted "a lot of em-phasis on quitting; at first that was very intimidating because I couldn't quit." Another commented, "The long-timers often made me feel like an outsider because I wasn't familiar with the lan-guage or buzzwords." Other problems included finding it hard to identify with other members, not knowing anyone, and finding the group to be "unsympathetic" and not God-centered. One woman said she wouldn't recommend GA because "a lot of times when you leave, you feel more like gambling than you did when you got there."

Although GA wasn't the answer for this small group of women, it's an important resource that is much more likely to be helpful than not helpful. If you find yourself not having a positive experience at one meeting, you can always try a different meeting, as GA groups tend to feel different depending on who is attending the meetings. Or you may decide to use other resources to stop gambling, which will be the subject of the next three chapters.

Ongoing Participation in Gamblers Anonymous

For the women who used the GA program, continuing participation remained important to them even after many years of abstinence. About three-fourths of the women reported they still attend GA meetings: in the last year, 42 percent attended once a week and 36 percent two or more times a week.[14]

Some people accuse GA (and other Twelve Step groups) of becoming "just a substitute addiction." Even if that is true, there is no denying that the consequences of regular GA attendance are usually healthier habits—no comparison to the devastation of a gambling addiction. And it may not be well understood that continued attendance at GA is a positive choice for several reasons:

1. To participate in sponsorship of other women
2. To give back ("What would have happened to me if I'd gone to GA and no one was there?")
3. To hear people talk about the consequences of their gambling and remind you why you quit ("I needed to hear people's pain, I needed to hear about the people who went to jail, I needed to hear about people whose marriages broke up, because sometimes you feel like you're invulnerable")

4. To continue to develop along spiritual lines as suggested in the Twelve Steps

"Working the Steps"

"Working the Twelve Steps" is part of ongoing participation of GA. It is considered by many to be the backbone of maintaining a gambling-free life and becoming a better person. "Working the Steps" is not a mysterious process, although it may seem that way to newcomers in the program. In general, it means reading about and discussing the meaning of each Step with a sponsor or in a "Step Meeting"—meetings with that specific focus. At some point, to "work the Step" means to embrace its message and to take some action as a commitment to that belief. Gamblers Anonymous publishes a pamphlet, *Working the Steps,* that explains their general meaning and gives suggestions on how to work on them.[15]

What follows is a brief general explanation of each Step and recommended actions as outlined by the pamphlet and as interpreted by some of the women in the Internet study and by other commentators. The process of "working the Steps" is similar in all Twelve Step programs, so some of the commentators focus on that process in general, not just in GA. This information is not intended to substitute for the actual experience of going to meetings, working with a sponsor, and taking actions recommended by GA members.

Step One

"We admitted we were powerless over gambling—that our lives had become unmanageable."

Step One is the cornerstone of recovery for gamblers who are trying to get well through the GA program. Powerlessness over gambling is usually self-evident to the families of compulsive gamblers or to people aware of what may be a largely secret life. However, according to GA literature, the gambler herself typically harbors a fantasy that she can someday gamble "normally" like everyone else. That belief "has to be smashed" in order to work Step One.[16]

Some women and other professionals get concerned about the language of "powerlessness," because women as a group are already more powerless than men in the dominant culture.[17] They fear that the notion of powerlessness reinforces the belief that a woman must submit to something (such as a power greater than herself) or someone (something she may have done all her life in a secular sense). An answer for this criticism lies in an understanding of what "powerless *over gambling*" really means.

The *Working the Steps* pamphlet has a riveting description in the section on Step One:

■■■ *We believed, at one time or another, that all of our problems could be solved with a big win. Some, pathetically, even after making a big win, found themselves in worse trouble within a short period of time. We continued to gamble. We found we had risked loss of family, friends, security and jobs. We still continued to gamble. We gambled to the point where it resulted in imprisonment, insanity or attempted suicide. We still continued to gamble and were unable to stop . . . Many times we swore we would not gamble again, believing we had the will-power to stop gambling. We believed a lie.*[18] ■■■

Honestly facing the hard fact of being out of control with gambling, no matter what you try to do, and having your life in various stages of shambles around you ("My life is unmanageable") roughly translates to the understanding of "powerlessness" in Step One. For creating even more understanding, the pamphlet recommends an action step: write out your specific answers to each of the Twenty Questions (see pages 31–32).

Jodi had been in the GA program for over a year before she started working on the Steps. She found help in Patrick Carnes's book *A Gentle Path Through the Twelve Steps: The Classic Guide for All People in the Process of Recovery*.[19] She says, "Just working on the First Step really thoroughly with that book showed me how important this is going to be to me. I can feel the difference in my general attitude, just going through this one part, and I haven't even gotten to the nitty-gritty of a Fourth Step inventory."

Step Two

"Came to believe that a Power greater than ourselves could restore us to a normal way of thinking and living."

This Step tells the person that there is a solution to their gambling problem, and that solution is "living a spiritual recovery program."[20] The GA program offers a lot of leeway on just what that spiritual recovery may look like. Some women use their sponsor, or the GA group as a whole, to give them the guidance for restoring normality to their lives. For example, Mary "had a problem with the idea of God." She says that it took her a long time to even be able to say the words "Higher Power." But she was able to work Step Two because she accepted that "the power of the GA group was tremendous," and that it could restore her to sanity. Others come to believe in a Higher Power that may be a Christian God, Buddha, Nature, or whatever leads us toward a less self-centered view of the world. An action step recommended in the *Working the Steps* pamphlet is to practice keeping an open mind and be mindful of our fixed beliefs.

Step Three

"Made a decision to turn our will and our lives over to the care of this Power of our own understanding."

This Step emphasizes that GA is a spiritual fellowship, not a religious one. The idea is to connect with the healing energy (grace, Godness) of the world and/or within oneself and become receptive to spiritual guidance. The *Working the Steps* pamphlet advises that "a Higher Power and you walking side by side can work together each day so that you can become better than you have ever been."[21]

For Brenda, the decision in Step Three was to form such a partnership. She says, "My Higher Power is a huge part of my recovery. I call my Higher Power God, He, She, or It, it doesn't matter. But I look at that relationship as a partnership with God, who is the senior partner . . . As long as I remember who is senior, then things go well. I trust my ability to make well-reasoned decisions now, which I never had [before]. When I make a decision I'm confident that I was supposed to decide that way, and it might not always work out as I expect—often it doesn't. But it's working out the way my Higher Power wants it to work out."

Step Four

"Made a searching and fearless moral and financial inventory of ourselves."

This is the "clean house" Step. GA recommends a thorough reading of the *Fourth Step Inventory Moral Book* (available through the GA Online Store for around $1.00), for this important Step. The GA *Working the Steps* pamphlet also suggests that you start by writing an autobiography of your gambling, beginning with your first bet to the present. In the process, you are likely to become more aware of areas of "guilt, over-indulgence, greed, lying, dishonesty, failure to accept responsibility, self-destruction,

destruction of others, excessive waste of time, arrogance, resentment, jealousy and many others."[22] Obviously, this can be a painful process; it was dreaded by some of the women in the Internet study. However, according to GA, these past transgressions must be fully realized and dealt with, so that these painful memories and regrets don't push you into gambling again. The action Step is to write it all down, as honestly as possible. Needless to say, this is an important time to have a sponsor to lean on.

For Tara, working through the Fourth Step helped her get to know herself in a whole new way:

> ■■■ Working the Steps is hard to do. It was hard to grasp the whole meaning of each Step. There is a lot more to it than just what it says. And it's hard work facing all the things that you've done and facing your past and seeing your character flaws. It's meeting yourself for the first time, really. That's what it boiled down to for me. I'm still doing it. But I had a lot of support; I mean I had a sponsor who made me slow down, made me take the time to really do introspective work.
>
> Step Four, in particular, was real hard. It took me about four months to do it. I already knew what most of the issues were, the big issues that went all the way back to my childhood. So identifying the issues was easy. Mostly. But journaling about it, and then looking at it from a different perspective, was really enlightening. It was also kind of maddening because it made me see my part in everything, and I couldn't just blame it all on somebody else. ■■■

Step Five

"Admitted to ourselves and to another human being the exact nature of our wrongs."

There are no easy cures to guilt and remorse about our past mistakes. However, with solace, care, and support from other people,

we can help each other through difficult experiences that are sometimes excruciatingly painful. That is the purpose of Step Five. By
talking honestly to another human being about our failures, we can
lighten our burden and begin the process of becoming more humble
and compassionate toward others who have made mistakes. The
honest sharing required in Step Five is a powerful antidote to the
gambling days, when our habits were lying and hiding from problems, and acting as a "loner." When looking for a person to hear
your Fifth Step, the *Working the Steps* pamphlet suggests finding
someone who "has the wisdom to help you see the situation more
clearly, and be a person who will keep the conversation completely
confidential."[23] Women in the Internet survey read their Fourth
Step inventory to their sponsors, clergy, or counselors to complete
Step Five.

Kevin Griffin, in *One Breath at a Time: Buddhism and the
Twelve Steps,* writes that a common revelation in the Fifth Step
process is to learn you are not alone, that your mistakes are shared
by many, and that you do not need to be mired down in shame
and remorse.[24] Author Stephanie Covington says she was worried about what her AA sponsor would think of her after hearing
about what she had done in the past. In *A Woman's Way through
the Twelve Steps,* she writes:

■ ■ ■ *To my surprise, I felt tremendous relief when I did my Fifth Step.
My sponsor accepted me just as I was, secrets and all. She didn't
judge me. Instead, she listened and understood. For me, this was
a giant step out of isolation and toward a sense of belonging. By
receiving uncritical acceptance from another woman, I began to
accept myself and let go of the guilt and remorse I'd carried for so
long.*[25] ■ ■ ■

Step Six

"Were entirely ready to have these defects of character removed."

After searching out your defects and negative emotions, and admitting them to another person, Step Six is the beginning of working on and eliminating them. The purpose is very practical—it's the path to a more serene life that will support your recovery and not lead you back to gambling. The action recommended is to make a list of your character defects and become ready and willing to do something about them.

Step Seven

"Humbly asked God (of our understanding) to remove our shortcomings."

We have already let go of our destructive relationship to gambling. Now this Step asks us to let go of destructive habits that may lead us back into gambling and keep us from living a good life. Naturally, that doesn't happen all at once, so many people in Twelve Step programs look at this as a "process Step." Jodi views Step Seven as "where the real work is." She says, "Gambling was just my medication; the character defects are the real stuff." The *Working the Steps* pamphlet puts it very simply: "When you leave the world of reality and slip into irrational anger, you should now be able to recognize that something is wrong. You now have to get yourself back on the right track so you can go deal with today. Anger could lead you back to a bet via the hatred and resentment created."[26] A practical way to deal with Step Seven is to make it part of your morning ritual: select one "defect" to work on that day, and ask for help from your Higher Power to reduce or remove it.

Step Eight

"Made a list of all persons we had harmed and became willing to make amends to them all."

The action for this Step is making a list of those people we had harmed through such things as stealing, lying, abandoning, betraying, scaring, or however we were "abusing others or taking from them the right to lead their own lives."[27] Most compulsive gamblers have a painful personal history with their family, friends, and loved ones, not to mention creditors and employers. Looking deeply at the pain we have caused others helps to soften our own heart and build compassion.

Step Nine

"Make direct amends to such people wherever possible, except when to do so would injure them or others."

It's very helpful to have a sponsor to guide you through this Step and determine the meaning of "direct amends" and "wherever possible." In general, the Step requires that you take responsibility for your part in whatever caused pain and suffering. In particular, this could mean such actions as acknowledging and repaying money you stole out of someone's purse, anonymously donating to a charity in someone's name if you can't find the person, making a face-to-face apology and payback plan with your sister for your demands to borrow more and more money, apologizing to your teenage daughter for not being available to her during her high school years, and so on.

Many wonder how making amends could "injure them or others." It's possible to be overenthusiastic about this Step and to needlessly disclose incidents that are better left unsaid, and will only hurt the person. Another example of potential harm was described by Linda, whose father was a compulsive gambler: "He was a person that I borrowed a lot of money from. I couldn't pay him back because it would go straight into the machine." As an alternative, she invited her dad to live with her toward the end of his life. "He lived there free for quite a while because of the money I owed him."

Completing Step Nine can put an end to the terrible isolation suffered by most compulsive gamblers, reconnecting them in an honest way to those they have avoided or hidden from. However, sometimes it is not possible to mend the relationship. The person you've hurt is too angry to accept your amends at that time, or perhaps has been burned by believing in you before, only to watch you return to gambling and your old ways. It could even be that the person you've hurt has done you damage, and you think maybe that person should be making amends to you! Regardless of these considerations, the amends still need to be made. The advice from old-timers in Twelve Step programs is to "clean up your side of the street." As GA says about this Step: "Abstaining from gambling, working the program and making amends, you will gradually return to society. Self-respect, so long absent, starts to return."[28]

Step Ten

"Continued to take personal inventory and when we were wrong, promptly admitted it."

The last three Steps—Ten, Eleven, and Twelve—are commonly understood as the "maintenance Steps". For Step Ten, a daily inventory of how we have approached our day is recommended. How did we treat others? Did we help anyone? Were we generous with anyone? Were we able to keep a lid on our tendency to "boil over" when frustrated? How did we handle a difficult decision? Did we promptly admit we were wrong when it became quite obvious, even to us, that we were? What do we need to work on for tomorrow? In her inventory, Elise looked for these signs that told her she was slipping out of her recovery program: "When

I start losing my temper, when I get impatient, when I snap at people, when things are irritating me that shouldn't irritate me, and when I start minding other people's business instead of my own." Getting into the habit of reviewing our behaviors at the end of the day can help us not only spot warning signs, but also become aware of the personal growth we have made. A helpful slogan for this Step might be "Progress, not perfection."

Step Eleven

"Sought through prayer and meditation to improve our conscious contact with God as we understood Him, praying only for knowledge of His will for us and the power to carry that out."

Just as Step Ten asks us to maintain and make progress on our emotional growth, Step Eleven asks us to do the same in the spiritual realm. A daily prayer (such as the Serenity Prayer) or practice (such as meditation) is recommended. The idea is to take time out every day to turn inward—away from the distractions of relationships, work, and worldly responsibilities—and take stock of where you are with your spiritual life. It's a chance to nourish your spiritual connection and seek guidance on getting you through your day.

Step Twelve

"Having made an effort to practice these principles in all our affairs, we tried to carry this message to other compulsive gamblers."

Traditionally, Step Twelve is viewed as the service Step. We are asked to be of service to others. In the GA program itself, service can mean setting up chairs for the meeting, making coffee, sponsoring other gamblers, calling on a member who is sick, chatting after meetings with new members, running a meeting, or performing any of the other necessary tasks to keep the GA program running smoothly. In the wider world, practicing the principles of the program can mean "giving back" to whoever needs you, whenever they need you, such as volunteering for soup kitchens, helping out with Little League, reading to elders, and so on. As the GA *Working the Steps* pamphlet puts it, "If you give of yourself and try to help another human being, you will gain from the act of giving even if your effort fails."[29]

It has probably become clear to you, after reading this brief explanation of the Twelve Steps that "working the Steps" can be a lifelong effort and way of life. The results can be dramatic, from finding a spiritual life where there was none, to starting each day with hope instead of despair. There are also likely to be more subtle effects. Here's the way Stephanie describes it: "It made me a better person all the way around. When I first got into recovery and my husband would ask me a question (usually about a bill or where I was or whatever), I would catch myself lying. And now I turn back around and say—you know what? That was not true, this is the truth. I used to have to practice telling the truth. Today, I don't have to practice."

Melanie has sponsored many women in her years of recovery. She recommends going to "Step meetings" that focus on a particular Step every month. She says, "the people who are attending them are staying clean, and they know what working the Steps is all about. It's not just reading them out of the Combo Book, it's doing them, it's living them, it's taking them home, it's taking them to work, and it's taking them out on the freeway. I mean I was a bad driver before GA. I wanted to get out there and run everybody off the road, flip them off and do everything my way. But today I am a little more careful and I respect other people's rights on the freeway."

Sponsorship

Unlike Alcoholics Anonymous, which has a deep well of women who have attended AA for years and worked through the Steps, Gamblers Anonymous has only recently begun to attract women in numbers. Consequently, finding a female sponsor experienced in GA Twelve Step work can be problematic. This may explain why sponsorship of other women was an important part of GA participation for most of the Internet survey respondents who continued to attend GA. Of those answering this question, 63 percent had sponsored someone in GA, and the average number of women sponsored was almost four. One woman with almost twenty years of recovery reported sponsoring over 100 women in the program.

Sponsors are available to help a new person understand the GA program and help them work the Twelve Steps. Generally, sponsors provide much more than this. They can be a shoulder to cry on, a person to call when the urge to gamble feels overwhelming, and a listening ear when no one else seems to care. Sometimes, a woman from the meeting volunteers to be a temporary sponsor to a newcomer still looking for the right permanent sponsor. However, the most common way to find a sponsor in GA or any Twelve Step program is to ask someone who seems like a good fit with you. You generally look for someone who has abstinence time, has preferably "worked the Steps," and attends meetings regularly.

When female sponsors are not available within GA, some women have reached out to Alcoholics Anonymous members for help working on the Steps; others recruited male GA sponsors, although this is not recommended. Susan got around the potential problem of having a male sponsor by asking his wife's permission and maintaining contact with her.

Sponsorship is not always "official." Although Sandy has a person in Alcoholics Anonymous who is her official sponsor, she and another friend in GA "sponsor each other every day." Sandy says, "She can see things and put me back on the right track, when I didn't want to see it." Helen tells about getting to know her future sponsor at a GA meeting—a relationship that became the most helpful thing in her recovery process:

■■■ *There was a girl who came, and she was younger than I was, but she had a lot of time [in recovery]. She already was going on her fifth year. She was a professional gambler, and she had tried suicide. I finally heard her story all at once. She welcomed me so much, and she had so much love, that I asked her to be my sponsor. She hasn't been really hard on me and pushing me to do the Steps, because she knows that I did the Steps in the Al-Anon program, and did my Fifth Step and a lot of my Steps with my counselor. I still have her as a sponsor, and when I don't go to a meeting because I don't feel good, she calls me up and says "Where were you?" She is a very loving person.* ■■■

"Women Preferred" Meetings

Why not just say "women's meetings"? Because the principles of Gamblers Anonymous state that "the only requirement for membership is a desire to stop gambling." Officially, no one who has that desire can be excluded from a GA meeting. But word gets around, and pretty soon you have both "women preferred" and "men preferred" meetings, as in Everett, Washington.

The development of such meetings began in 1992, when Marilyn L. started a "women preferred" GA meeting in Arizona. Although it struggled in the beginning, by 1999 there were three "women preferred" meetings in the Phoenix area. Many other states now have them, such as the one started by Jane R. in Yale-New Haven, Connecticut, in 1994, and the one begun in Amityville, New York, in 2007. Check the GA website to see if you have one in your area.

There are many potential benefits to attending a "women preferred" GA meeting. According to Marilyn, "There are issues women can't talk about in front of men, very personal, like maybe child abuse, or sexual or physical abuse by a husband or [another] man. We became more honest there because we weren't using our wiles to flirt with the men. It's not that we don't like men. It's just that we don't identify with all their issues, and they don't identify with ours. How many men have said, 'I just don't understand women!'"

Pauline offers this rationale for needing a women's meeting:

■■■ *Most of us, as women, have had a lifetime of survival and one of the ways to survive is to subtly manipulate men. Women see through that with other women. When you are with just women, you don't have to deal with hiking your skirt up. I think you cut through a lot of that in a women's group. There are women who don't want to be in women's groups because they know all that goes out the window . . . [but] there are just so many things you can talk about openly with men there. In a women's meeting, you're not opening the door for guys to hit on you if they know you are having marital problems.* ■■■

Will GA Work for Me?

The responses to the Internet survey make it clear that most women attending GA are having a positive experience, primarily in mixed-gender meetings. Perhaps because more women are attending, the stories in meetings now include not only the "high-roller" type of gambling but also the types of gambling more women participate in, such as slots and video poker. It is also likely that new female members can now find other women to ask for help—thus avoiding asking for help from a man, which is sometimes misinterpreted as a sexual come-on. The stereotype of GA as a male preserve, unfriendly to females, is no longer the dominant story, even though pockets of gender bias still remain. The women on the Internet survey listed many ways in which GA and its members supported their recovery. For example:

- "Accepting me the way I was and letting me hang on and learn however much I needed. Being there for me night and day in the beginning, inviting me along."
- "Just having someone to talk to about the past gambling and helping me remember how bad it was."
- "Telling me I could quit, that I am a good person."
- "Understanding without blaming . . . encouragement, praise for my continuing abstinence."
- "Introducing me to the Twelve Steps."
- "Believing in the possibility of recovery and my ability to get it."
- "Listening to their stories and being able to tell mine . . . seeing people succeed by getting their coins [medallions for "abstinence anniversaries"] and seeing the newcomers fresh from the casino. Their stories tell me it is still hell out there and I am doing the right thing by staying away from all gambling."

At a minimum, the members of GA can offer acceptance to individuals who are usually isolated from their families and shamed by their inability to stop gambling. The program offers hope that recovery is always possible. For these reasons alone, it's worth trying out a few meetings of GA to see if it's a good fit for you.

GA's Sister: Gam-Anon

Gam-Anon is a mutual-help Twelve Step program for spouses, family, and friends of compulsive gamblers. (In the parallel world of Alcoholics Anonymous, Al-Anon is the same kind of program.) The purpose of Gam-Anon is to help individuals involved with a compulsive gambler find help with the devastation, bitterness, resentment, stress, and tension that comes with that relationship while the gambler is "out practicing." Gam-Anon is founded on spiritual principles, with a purpose of creating and preserving serenity in the lives of their members. Like GA, it is not affiliated with Christianity or any other organized religious group. Meetings are run by people who are in relationships with compulsive gamblers, not by professional facilitators. The members offer practical suggestions for living with or without the compulsive gambler and guides for building and maintaining a more satisfying and spiritual life. Its official Web site at www.gam-anon.org offers practical suggestions for newcomers and a schedule of meetings by state.

Gam-Anon Suggestions for the Newcomer

1. *Accept and learn to live with the fact that compulsive gambling is an illness.*
2. *To question or interrogate the gambler will serve no purpose. You are powerless over this situation. If the gambler has something the gambler wishes to hide, the truth cannot be forced from the gambler. Why try?*
3. *To nag your gambler about past losses or to talk of what might have been if the gambler hadn't gambled will prove to be detrimental to the gambler's recovery as well as yours.*

Suggestions for the Newcomer is reprinted from the official Gam-Anon Web site, www.gam-anon.org, with permission.

4. The past is gone and you will not find peace of mind until you can accept it without resentment.

5. The gambler, not you, should be responsible for calling the gambler's creditors to make restitution. Don't take this responsibility from the gambler.

6. Experience has taught us that it is not helpful to borrow monies or co-sign notes to cover gambling debts, while the gambler is gambling or when the gambler comes into Gamblers Anonymous.

7. It is not recommended that the spouse go to work specifically to cover gambling debts.

8. Prudence tells us that compulsive gamblers are seldom able to handle family finances. Perhaps this condition will be altered as the gambler progresses toward recovery.

9. Discourage friends and relatives from lending the gambler money.

10. Gamblers Anonymous is a program for the compulsive gambler. Loved ones should not interfere.

11. It may be well to encourage the gambler to go to the first few meetings, however, after this the Gamblers Anonymous activities must be left to the gambler. To force the gambler to attend meetings is very apt to do more harm than good.

12. The gambler's gambling debts were not incurred over a short period of time, therefore don't be discouraged if the gambler finds it necessary to pay back small amounts of monies over an extended period. Normal family expenses must come first.

13. Recovery is a very slow process for the gambler. Give the gambler your encouragement and have faith.

14. Do take an honest inventory of YOUR character defects and work on them.

15. Come to Gam-Anon even though your gambler may continue to gamble. We understand your problem and if you have an honest desire we can help you through our program.

Gam-Anon Participation and Support

Historically, Gam-Anon has been the preserve of the wives of male gamblers. There used to be a joke in research circles that women have indeed been studied in the problem gambling arena, it's just that they've all been in Gam-Anon, not GA! Since Gam-Anon as an organization does not keep national records of attendance, there is no way to determine the actual participation of men or women. The 1999 edition of the GA-authored book *Sharing Recovery Through Gamblers Anonymous* notes that "the majority of Gam-Anon members are wives of compulsive gamblers, since most members of GA are married males."[30] Since the actual membership of GA is rapidly changing to include more females, it is reasonable to predict that Gam-Anon membership is also changing to include more husbands and other male family members.

At the time they filled out the Internet survey, only 8 percent of the women currently had relatives or friends attending Gam-Anon, and only 29 percent said that their gambling had ever prompted relatives or friends to attend. What effect did Gam-Anon attendance seem to have? Of these women, about two-thirds thought it was helpful or very helpful for the relative, and about one-third said it had no effect at all or was not helpful. Suzie says that Gam-Anon "helped my spouse to understand the illness and helped him see his own character defects and his contribution to my gambling, such as ignoring the symptoms because he didn't want to face the problem either." Brenda says it was helpful for her husband to attend because it reinforced actions she needed to take to stop her gambling. She explains, "I learned in GA that I should turn over my credit cards, checks, and ATM cards. . . . My husband, although he knew I should, didn't make me. When he first went to Gam-Anon he was told this was necessary. . . . This was helpful because I no longer could get enough money to go to the casinos without his knowledge."

A woman who attended a GA conference that had Gam-Anon

members mentioned one other positive effect: "It was very diffi-cult to listen to the pain that was done to them by 'the gamblers.' Up to that point, I had not realized the impact my actions had on my family." Although not directly related to Gam-Anon, Julie experienced a benefit when she started taking her husband and daughter to open GA meetings. She says, "I think it decreases the amount of judgment they place on me. They get to see more of the illness and what the illness does."

Only a few women whose friends or relatives had attended Gam-Anon found the experience was not helpful to their own recovery. "He used Gam-Anon to enhance his righteousness," Susan commented. Elsa said, "The Gam-Anon group here mostly was a whining session, and no one was facilitating in such a way that they were actually following a program."

Because the Internet research survey focused on women with gambling problems, Gam-Anon was only reviewed from their per-spective. To find out more about this resource for families, check out the pamphlets from the Gam-Anon International Service Office found at www.gam-anon.org, or search an online bookstore such as amazon.com for related titles.

Becoming involved with Gamblers Anonymous was a pivotal part of the recovery process for most of the women in the Internet survey. For a few, the involvement of their significant others in the Gam-Anon program was an additional aid to their recovery. But there were also women who found that GA was not enough, or that it didn't fulfill their needs. Some of them went on to seek professional help, which is the focus of the next chapter.

CHAPTER 7

Professional Help

"Professional help helps you to get over the devastation of you going through shame, you going through guilt, you going through humiliation, you going through alienation from your family, your friends, and anybody that cares about you." ■■■ **Sarah, age 42**

T he decision to seek professional help for a problem is usually not our first choice. Most people who find themselves with troubles initially reach out to more informal resources such as family, close friends, trusted clergy, even Internet resources. When these resources fail and our troubles are still with us, we start to see the need to access help beyond our more intimate circle.

For many women with gambling problems, informal resources to help with their problems are no longer readily available. Families are alienated or frustrated with trying to help, money is owed to friends, and the clergy, like most people, may not understand a gambling problem. At the same time, everything is getting worse. Excessive gambling in and of itself can lead to depression, thoughts of suicide, fractured relationships, and rock-bottom self-esteem. In addition, past and present issues of emotional and/or physical abuse, difficult family-of-origin issues, fragile temperaments, relationship problems, and loneliness can fuel the urge to escape these unhappy feelings through more gambling. Current studies indicate that both men and women with gambling problems may also experience a range of other problems diagnosed in the *DSM-IV-TR*, such as an alcohol use disorder (73 percent), personality disorder (61 percent), nicotine dependence (60 percent), mood disorder (50 percent), anxiety disorder (41 percent), and drug use disorder (38 percent).[1]

Because women with a gambling problem usually have other problems as well, and because informal resources are either nonexistent or inadequate, professional help may become a necessary option. For the women in the Internet study, two types of professional treatment were found helpful: inpatient treatment focused on stopping gambling problems, and outpatient treatment focused on gambling and difficult life problems that become more apparent and pressing in recovery. This chapter describes the women's experience in both types. It also delves into the beliefs that drive the two most common treatment models that are used in gambling treatment, briefly describes the use of medication, and ends with a look at how to find qualified professional help.

Gambling Treatment for Women

Until recently, women did not access gambling treatment nearly as much as men. However, as the number of female gamblers has grown, and their problems have escalated, treatment programs have been seeing many more of them. In a 2004 interview with the online resource WebMD, prominent researcher Nancy Petry, Ph.D., reported, "What is striking is that ten or fifteen years ago, 95 percent of the people in treatment for gambling were men. Now it's 60 percent men and 40 percent women. Programs all over the United States and Canada are seeing this."[2]

States are beginning to fund treatment programs with the profits they make from gambling, and the certification process for gambling counselors is ensuring more trained professionals. Even so, there are still numerous barriers to getting professional help:

- Finding professional treatment specifically for gambling problems can be more difficult than finding alcohol or drug treatment. Thirty states fund some type of gambling-related service—but that might mean a referral hotline, rather than actual treatment programs. Funding levels are low, and treatment programs solely for women gamblers don't exist in the United States or Canada.

- Paying for treatment may also be problematic. Most insurance companies still exclude gambling treatment from mental health benefits, even though alcohol/ drug problems and mental health issues are covered, and even though pathological gambling is listed as a mental health diagnosis in the *DSM-IV-TR*.

- Sometimes a woman just doesn't know that professional help is available for gambling problems, and if she does know about it, she may think it's only for women with more serious problems than hers, or she may fear she will be the only woman there.

In spite of these potential barriers, 42 percent of the women in the Internet study reported that they received some type of professional help to stop gambling, deal with the problems caused by gambling, and/or deal with the problems that gambling had enabled them to temporarily escape. About 11 percent used therapy or counseling services not specific to gambling; a smaller fraction attended an inpatient or outpatient gambling treatment program, and a few women tried drug or alcohol counseling or worked with a psychiatrist, religious-based counselor, or hypnotist.[3]

Types of Professional Treatment

Several types of professional help are available, each with a point of view about the causes of gambling problems.

The Cognitive-Behavioral Therapy Model: Gambling Is a Bad Habit, Not a Disease

According to cognitive-behavioral therapy (CBT), gambling problems develop because of maladaptive thinking and unhealthy habits. The basic idea is that our thinking causes our feelings and behaviors. The key to successful treatment, then, is relearning and rethinking old patterns that don't work anymore. Treatment success in the CBT model occurs when clients attain the goals they have set for themselves. Therapists trained in this approach emphasize that moderating or stopping a person's gambling activity is a matter of personal choice. Often the goal is to stop altogether, but a goal of moderate gambling without negative consequences is also acceptable.

The cognitive-behavioral model is very helpful in understanding how thinking and habitual behaviors can lead people to continue to gamble even when the results are bad for them. For example, when Susan had an urge to gamble, "I always told myself that this time I'll win—after all, I had already poured so much money into those machines." Susan persists in the notion, despite all evidence to the contrary, that she will ultimately win and recuperate her lost money—because of her irrational cognitions and the behavioral conditioning patterns that have occurred over time at the casino.

Behaviorists call it "intermittent reinforcement," the strongest type of conditioning that makes us want to continue a behavior regardless of its overall costs. That is because, every once in a while, our brain gets a big shot of reinforcement to do so. Let's see how this might work if you're a new gambler playing an electronic slot-machine game.

The first time you go to a casino, someone tells you that the Sun and Moon game is a fun one. The object is to get certain combinations of five suns or moons to come up on the slot-machine screen at once. When a whole row of suns or moons comes up, it starts a bonus round of fifty free games, which can lead to many more points, more winning spins, and even more points. You sit down with your forty dollars and start betting cautiously. After about fifteen spins, the right combination of suns and moons comes up, and you're into bonus points and extra spins—and soon you're up $175. Your brain, which constantly and naturally is scanning for patterns, tells you: *This is a winning machine—so do more!* You start betting more and begin to lose. After you've lost $100, you decide to go home, feeling good about your ability to pick the right machine.

The next five times you come to the casino, you go back to the same machine, but nothing exciting happens—you win a little but mostly lose. However, your brain has picked up a pattern: after about twenty spins, you win at least something. On your sixth visit, you try another machine and all it does is lose. Your brain tells you something is bound to happen soon, so you step away to withdraw some more cash from the ATM. When you get back, an elderly woman in a walker has taken over your machine and is placing fifty-cent bets. You start to tell her that it is "your machine," but suddenly all five suns come up and she's won a big one. While you kick yourself for leaving, your brain files away another valuable lesson, which is: *Never give up.*

The next time you come to the casino, you are prepared. You have $500 from a payday loan, confident that this time you will have enough to win and pay off the loan tomorrow with no penalty. You start playing the original machine that won for you. Very methodically, you place two-dollar bets. Nothing happens. You raise your bet to $2.50. Still nothing happens, and now you're going down fast. You've put so much money in that there is no way you are going to leave this machine for another little old lady to come and cash in on your money.

You are finally down to your last ten dollars. Ten bucks is useless compared to your debt, so you decide to bet five dollars on the last two bets. You push the button for the first bet, and nothing happens. You light a cigarette, take a drink of Coke, and swear you will never come back if you can only win something on your last bet. You push the button and *all five suns* come up in a row, the highest bonus of all! On your five-dollar bet you rake in $1,500. You feel vindicated! Now you have the real secret! Your brain has been reinforced to the new rule: *When you're down, keep on playing and eventually you'll hit a big one!* Your brain has been hard-wired now by the intermittent reinforcement of a big win. Unfortunately, this rule takes precedence over the rational part of your brain that would tell you, if asked, that by continuing to gamble you will inevitably lose much more than you ever have the possibility of winning. That's why casinos make money and build golf courses and hotels.

CBT is designed to help you develop strategies to deal with intermittent reinforcement and the erroneous thoughts stored in your brain that tell you to keep on gambling. This model of gambling treatment is more widely used in its pure form in Canada, but elements of it are also used in the United States. Most U.S. treatment programs offer a variety of behavioral techniques, such as:

1. *Contingency contracting.* The gambler schedules affordable rewards for short periods of gambling abstinence (a cheap movie, an hour in an art gallery with a friend, a long bike ride, or a walk in the forest), and uses them continuously to build up abstinence time.
2. *Implementing behavioral barriers.* The gambler turns personal checks and credit cards over to the care of someone else; she bans herself from the casino.

3. *Imaginal desensitization exercises.* After a relaxation exercise, the gambler imagines increasingly arousing gambling scenes, each of which is followed by more relaxation. This helps give the person an alternative behavior (relaxation) when cravings to gamble start up. In another variation, the gambler imagines alternative choices for when the urge to gamble hits. For example, instead of cashing her paycheck at the bank and immediately going to the casino, she imagines (over and over) depositing all but twenty dollars of it and going with a friend to a movie.

The cognitive parts of CBT focus on the irrational thinking that is typical of compulsive gamblers. Irrational thinking is not limited to gamblers—we all do it at times of stress, strong emotions, or when engaged in any activity where chance is a factor. People who fly-fish tend to remember the big fish they caught and not the number of hours they spent fruitlessly casting their lines; a student who just flunked a test without studying for it may irrationally blame the instructor instead. With gamblers, irrational thinking occurs when they think they can control the game of chance by using certain strategies that will increase their chances of winning.

The most common thinking error with gamblers is misunderstanding the phenomenon of randomness and the extent to which outcomes can be predicted. Many gamblers think, "I've put so much money in the machine, it's bound to hit!" In reality, all casino games—slots, cards, all of them—are games of chance where the winning combination is based on random events. Randomness cannot be predicted because each event is independent from the others, and has no link to previous or following events.

The authors of *Understanding and Treating the Pathological Gambler* explain the independence of turns in this way to their patients:

■ ■ ■ *Gamblers are asked to consider a ball machine within which there is one sole red ball among 1000 white balls. Gamblers imagine that they are betting on their chances of drawing the red ball with their eyes covered. If, in their mind, they draw a white ball, we ask them to put the ball back and to bet again. Are gamblers closer to drawing the red ball after 3000 consecutive draws? Since the game resets after each draw, gamblers understand that each time they draw, they only have one out of 1000 chances of winning; even after betting 300 times, their chances of drawing the red ball remain the same.[4]* ■ ■ ■

Although it's extremely difficult for a compulsive gambler to give up the notion that the winning combinations of cards or slots can somehow be predicted, cognitive therapy teaches them that this is irrational thinking. Gamblers learn that it actually does no good to vary the speed of the bet, increase or decrease the size of the bet, or keep on betting with the notion that it finally has to hit after a certain time.

Other common thinking errors by problem gamblers include:

■ The personification of the gambling machines or dice (giving them human qualities and trying to influence them, such as gently rubbing a slot machine screen to coax out a win)

■ The "illusion of control" that certain conditions will increase the chance of winning, such as a choosing the right dealer or table, choosing a favorite slot machine, or walking into a casino through a certain entrance

■ The use of "flexible attributions," such as viewing losses as "near wins," and rationalizing a loss by identifying "fluke" events ("I knew I would start losing when the lights went out for a minute during the storm")

■ The use of the "availability bias": a person judges the probability of winning a jackpot based on the sounds of others winning or memories of past wins

■ Fixating on the "absolute frequency": gamblers will re-member the many times they win, without considering the relative number of losses ("I won five jackpots in the last two months!"). These are some of the common kinds of erroneous thoughts that keep gamblers thinking that they can control the game, predict results, and actually come out ahead.[5]

Counselors typically train problem gamblers to recognize their distorted thoughts and use strategies such as the "ABC of emotions" model to change such thoughts and the underlying beliefs. In this model, A stands for an activating event (such as waking up on 7/7/07), B stands for one's interpretation or belief about this event ("This is my lucky day!"), and C stands for the emotion, or consequence, of such an interpretation (I'm happily off to the ca-sino, anticipating a win). By reevaluating the B part of the model and changing the interpretation ("Today is just like any other day at the casino, and I'm likely to lose; therefore, I won't go") gam-blers can change their thoughts and the typical consequences of such thoughts.[6]

CBT programs in outpatient treatment centers in Canada usu-ally consist of ten to twelve sessions. In addition to the cognitive correction training described above, the menu of interventions usually includes financial planning, alternative activity planning, problem solving, communication training, and relapse prevention. Evaluations of CBT programs have found that this approach is ef-fective in reducing symptoms, cravings to gamble, and gambling frequency.[7] In a rare study of cognitive-behavioral treatment for nineteen women with electronic games problems, researchers found that at six months after treatment, 89 percent of them had reduced their symptoms to the point where they no longer met diagnostic criteria for pathological gambling.[8]

The Disease/Medical Model: Gambling Is a Disease, Not a Bad Habit

The disease/medical model of addiction is by far the most prevalent in the United States and has a long tradition of general public acceptance for treating alcohol and drug problems. The American Medical Association adopted the disease model for alcoholism in 1958, and it has been very successful in shifting the public perception of alcoholism from that of a moral failure to a treatable disease. Because many U. S. gambling treatment programs are added on to existing substance abuse treatment programs, and gambling counselors are likely to come from the ranks of substance abuse counselors, gambling treatment in the United States typically reflects the influence of the disease model of treatment.

The primary tenet of the disease model is that addiction (to alcohol, drugs, gambling, nicotine, and so on) is a *primary* disease; that is, it is the cause, rather than symptom, of other problems. In other words, your gambling addiction is your primary problem; when you fix that, other problems—such as depression, family disruption, finances, and so on—will then have a chance to clear up. If you don't fix the addiction, then these other problems won't get fixed either. Abstinence is critical in this model because of the belief that the disease of gambling addition can never be cured. It can, however, be arrested, as long as the person stays on guard against relapse and remains abstinent.

The disease model of treatment also differs from the cognitive-behavioral model in its close relationship to Twelve Step programs such as AA and GA. In the disease model, going to Gamblers Anonymous meetings and working on the Twelve Steps is encouraged. Some programs have patients begin Steps One, Two, and Three while in treatment. A spiritual component that is compatible with Twelve Step programs is frequently introduced. The use of recovering gamblers as peer counselors, in addition to the professional staff, is more common in programs working from a disease-model approach.

The first gambling inpatient program started in 1972 (and continues today) at the VA hospital in Brecksville, Ohio, and was patterned after the existing disease-model program for alcoholics. Typically, a disease-model program utilizes many strategies, including cognitive/behavioral techniques, family involvement, education about addiction, identifying family-of-origin issues, training in coping and problem-solving skills, relapse prevention, after-care planning, and individual and group therapy. Gambling-focused programs may also include financial counseling. Some of these strategies incorporate aspects of the cognitive-behavioral model, such as relapse prevention.

Attending to family-of-origin issues is a frequent strategy of disease-model treatment programs. In a strategy borrowed from substance abuse treatment, each patient writes an autobiography of significant gambling-related life events and then reads it to the group. Identifying and working on family-of-origin issues was helpful for Sharon in counseling. She says:

> ■■■ *I had to go all the way back and start with Mom. It was something that I didn't want to do. I felt like I had finally figured out that Mom did the best she could and I was finished with that, so I just didn't want to go there. So I did two hours of work related to my mother and just really finally getting to the core of that, beating the pillow and crying, and doing all that good stuff. I knew that was good work, because when I finished it and got in the car, I was done with it.* ■■■

Another helpful strategy used by treatment programs helps you look at the short- and long-term effects of your gambling. This chart shows the short- and long-term consequences of gambling—the seeming positives ("pros") and negatives ("cons"). It can be filled out individually, or with ideas offered by a treatment group. This sample shows some examples.

	Pros	**Cons**
Short-term Consequences	Escape from problems Hope of winning Anonymity Break from responsibilities Comfort of air conditioning Socializing Getting my fix	Losing money Hangovers Lying, sneaking No money for food Guilt and remorse Facing consequences Loss of self-esteem
Long-term Consequences	Hope of winning the big one	Broke, in debt Loss of relationships, family Isolation, depression Loss of job, car, house Loss of credibility Loss of trust Jail, prison Shame

Most gamblers who do this exercise see immediately that the benefits of gambling are all in the short term, and that the short- and long-term consequences of continuing to gamble are devastating. That's why many treatment programs stress that a deliberate pause to remember what happens *after* the gambling episode can help you put off the urge to gamble right now.

Another exercise common to both types of treatment is to write a letter to the problem. Externalizing the gambling problem by writing a "goodbye" letter helps to gain perspective on the grip that gambling has on you. Writing a "hello" letter to a new life without gambling puts some concrete rewards on paper that can be part of your future. Here's a real-life example from an interviewee:

Dear Gambling,

This is my good-bye letter to you, and a hello letter to a different way of life.

Goodbye, gambling, to the excitement of jumping in the car about 10 or 11 pm and heading out to the casino, looking forward to the crowds being gone and my favorite machines just sitting there waiting for me to choose the winner.

Goodbye to rolling down the window on a nice sunny day, blowing cigarette smoke out, turning up the radio, and thinking, ahhh . . . this is my lucky day, I'm due to win.

Goodbye to anxiously hurrying in from the parking lot, money in hand, hearing the casino noise, finding my favorite machine empty, and suddenly relaxing—I'm home.

Goodbye to the exhilaration of a winning run, when you know, you know, it's only going to get better every time you bet. Raising the bet to the maximum credits.

Goodbye to the sounds of the jackpot, the jolly tune, the lights blinking, the attention from other players, the slap of hundred-dollar bills that the attendants put in your hand. I knew it! I knew I was due for a win! Goodbye to the giddy feeling that now I can really relax and have fun, because it's their money I'm playing.

Goodbye to hiding in the restroom stall to count all my winnings, all those hundred-dollar bills, twenty-dollar bills, and putting most of the winnings in one pocket and the amount I'm prepared to lose in the other. Sorting it out, so I know I'm in control. Coming out of the restroom a winner, ready to win more.

Goodbye to sitting down to another machine, putting in $100 just for fun, I don't need this, I'm already a winner, then another $100, *and another $200, knowing it's got to start paying soon. Going into my winnings pocket for another $200, raising my bet to the limit because I know it's got to break real soon and I need a big payoff, another $200, goes fast at the highest bet, another $200, up but not enough to cover what I've lost, then down. What's wrong with this machine! The guy next to me is giving me looks, like he's sympathetic. He just wants me to leave so he can move over and win on my money! I'll show him I know what I'm doing when I get this jackpot. My last $200. Can't be much longer, this is crazy, I've never sat so long without it paying out, must be a really big one coming. Have to go to the ATM to get more money on the credit card. Leave my coat, and cigarettes, and ask the guy next to me to save my machine, as* I'll be back. *Just to let him know he won't be taking over anytime soon. Credit card maxed out. Hate that "Transaction declined." Have to go to the cashier, write a check for $500, my maximum. That should more than do it, won't be long and I'll be in the money. Have perfect credit at the casino, they won't check to see that I don't have any money in my account. It's just a loan, I'll easily have it back in the morning. Rush back, bump into people, and finally put another $200 in my machine. Must have gotten cold when I left. Another $200, not playing the max anymore, it goes up and down, and I get the feeling now that I won't win. I accept this. Even so, it could happen, and I put in the last $100, down to the last one credit. It's all gone.*

Goodbye to gathering up my coat and purse without looking at the guy next to me, walking out the door, smiling at the attendants as they say "Have a nice evening," finding my car, it's been so long I can't remember where I parked, opening the door, sitting down, and hating myself once again. Why couldn't I have quit when I was way ahead?!!!

What's wrong with me?!!!

Goodbye to telling myself all the way home, This is it! *Feeling a little bit of relief because I've blown it so bad I'll* have *to quit now. Figuring out how am I going to get out of this one. Figuring out how much more I can borrow from payday loans to cover the hot check. Not enough.*

Credit cards maxed out, one for $25,000, another $15,000 and six more than that. No more money to get out of a second mortgage on the house. Weighing the possibilities of asking a friend at work for a $600 loan—she's got the money easily—her husband basically supports her and she doesn't even have to work. Trying out the conversation in my head . . . What will I say? What can I say I need the money for?

Goodbye to crossing yet another line and borrowing a total of $3200 from friends and $1600 from my brother. Telling them each I've reached my bottom and this is the end, I'm going to GA every night. Instead, going to the casino as soon as they gave me the money. Can't quit now—I owe too much. Telling myself I'm due for another win, and this time I'll have sense enough to walk out.

Goodbye to opening the cupboard to see what I'll be able to eat for the next ten days until I get paid, and even then it won't get better because I have too much out in payday loans. Avoiding my friend at work because I can't pay her back when I said I would.

Goodbye to my pride that told me I could handle this on my own and I didn't need the bunch of losers in GA.

Hello to going back to another GA meeting, feeling welcomed like the prodigal daughter who finally came home again. Feeling ashamed but a little bit safer.

Hello to—in spite of all of that—gambling one more time. And losing. And another one more time. And yet another.

Hello to listening to people I used to write off as pontificators, male chauvinists, control freaks. Hello to hanging on to their every word.

Hello to going to meetings at least four times a week, maybe for the rest of my life.

Hello to getting through the worst two weeks. Hello to finally paying off the payday loans. Having money to buy food and gas.

Hello to seeing women come into GA who haven't lost what I have (emotionally, spiritually, relationships with children, and financially), and remembering that was where I was one year ago. Seeing them look at me the way I used to look at other people in GA, i.e., I'll never go that far. Now I'm the one who has gone that far. Hello to the new understanding in my gut that I have what it takes to go down even further.

Hello to quitting gambling now, not later (but not much later) when I've lost my car, house, job, and all the relationships I care about. Hello to letting go of regret for what I have already lost.

Hello to not working overtime to make money to supposedly pay debts, but in reality, using it to gamble more. Hello to taking naps, reading some spiritual books. Hello to going to see my grandchildren. Hello to GA sisters every day on the cell phone. Hello to possibilities I haven't even thought about for the last eight years that I've been gambling. Hello to Paris in 2010!

Hello to living every day without the crushing burden of my secret out-of-control gambling that put a barrier between me and every human being I encountered.

Hello to starting each day with the idea that I'm going to look for "Higher Power sightings," i.e., events or happenings that tell me there is a Power in human beings and in the natural world that extends itself for beauty, compassion, trust, and love beyond what one would normally expect. Sometimes it happens in an interaction with a coworker, sometimes it's the cold full moon, sometimes it's the cat curling herself under my chin at night and purring for no reason, sometimes it's a person crying and in despair at a GA meeting surrounded by people that understand.

Hello to a little bit of hope that with a lot of help I can get through today without gambling.

You don't have to be in a formal treatment program to write a goodbye letter to your gambling problem or a hello letter to your new life without gambling. One group of women who met regularly outside of GA or a treatment program used a variation: each member wrote a "divorce letter to gambling."

One of the side benefits of looking at addiction as a disease is that it justifies insurance coverage and may help people pay for treatment. Currently most insurance companies do not cover treatment for gambling problems, in spite of the fact that pathological gambling is named as a diagnosable disorder in the *DSM-IV-TR*. However, the disease/medical model approach was very successful in securing insurance coverage for alcohol and drug problems, so we can hope that perspective will carry over to gambling treatment in the near future.

Outcome studies on the effectiveness of treatment programs that use variations of the disease/medical model approach are full of the kinds of design and execution problems that cause research scientists much pain. One reason is that with so many types of strategies packed into these programs, it's hard to tease out which pieces are working and which aren't. In spite of the difficulties, several outcome studies report favorable results for the clients contacted, with abstinence rates of 40 to 60 percent.[9] A large study of six treatment programs in Minnesota (all with different variations of interventions) found that among those who had reported gambling once a week or more at intake, 40 percent were abstinent six months later, and 26 percent reported gambling less than once a month.[10]

Medication Treatments

Medication is not in itself a treatment for compulsive gambling. Although at this date there is no such thing as an approved "anti-gambling" medication, research studies have found that a number of medications can help gamblers in recovery in indirect ways.

Some people with gambling problems use medication to treat another coexisting problem such as depression, bipolar disorder, anxiety, or attention-deficit/hyperactivity disorder (ADHD). In these instances, the person may be prescribed mood stabilizers such as lithium and antidepressants. Others gamblers find that such medications help them deal with the difficult feelings that they may be trying to avoid through gambling—emotions such as shame, guilt, and anger. A chemically-induced "serenity" may provide enough relief that a person can focus on the problems that come up in recovery, such as relationship and financial issues. A third reason for using medication is to attempt to reduce cravings to gamble. These include such treatments as naltrexone, which is also used to reduce cravings in alcohol and drug addiction.[11]

In her article "Machines, Medication, Modulation: Circuits of Dependency and Self-Care in Las Vegas," Natasha Schull quotes a woman named Molly whom she met at a GA meeting. Molly told her: "A very common 'slip' when people read aloud from our book is: 'Sought through prayer and *medication*' (instead of *meditation*), which is laughable but truthful, because we have all self-medicated so much."[12] Perhaps Molly had noticed that gamblers may be attempting to self-medicate their depression, anxiety, ADHD symptoms, or substance abuse problems by using gambling as an escape.

The clinical trials to date have not identified an overwhelmingly successful medication for compulsive gamblers. But since many studies show that medication can improve a person's functioning—and problem gamblers, too, can benefit from these improvements—there is reason for optimism that in the future, more effective medications for problem gambling will be developed.[13]

Inpatient Treatment

A big benefit of inpatient treatment can simply be to remove the person from her gambling environment for a period of time, so she can reassess her situation. For Joni, this was the only real benefit of her first treatment experience.

Joni spent thirty days in an inpatient treatment program where she was the only person with gambling problems among about 120 people with alcohol or drug problems. The staff simply asked her to replace the program's content referring to "alcohol/drugs" with "gambling." The primary benefit of this treatment episode, according to Joni, was that "I just needed to get away; otherwise I would have been dead." She started gambling again within a month of leaving treatment, although not as much as before.

Three years and many hours of gambling later, Joni was the focus of an intervention organized by her mother, father, and sisters. A gambling intervention is generally an event planned by family members concerned about a compulsive gambler, together with a treatment professional. The participants confront the gambler with the reality of her situation and how it is affecting each family member. Treatment options are prearranged, so the gambler can choose to get immediate help. Joni recalls her experience of the event:

▪▪▪ *They told me to come over to their house, that they had some kind of rigged-up deal. When I got there, they were all sitting there with one of the counselor ladies and saying they wanted me to go to this gambling joint. [I answered,] I don't need help. I haven't been gambling like I was before. I don't need it now. So I thought about it for a couple of days and said, "Yeah, I do," and I went. It was one of the best things I ever did.* ▪▪▪

The second treatment episode, eighteen days at a different facility, was much more intense. There were only seven people in the program, and they all had gambling problems. As Joni describes it:

▪▪▪ *It was gambling only and they really knew their stuff. It was like they knew what they were talking about. You were up at eight and you were in different sessions all the way up until eight at night. Real intense, real intense. They set me up with a counselor in my area, and he was really, really good.* ■■■

Joni remained abstinent from gambling for six months, had three intermittent gambling lapses over a period of several months, and had maintained abstinence again for about eight months prior to her interview after the Internet survey. Her health insurance didn't cover either of the treatment programs, and she is still paying for one of them. She maintains, however, that the price is "nothing compared to the gambling."

Brenda is another woman who benefited from inpatient treatment focused on gambling. Because she is a veteran, she was eligible to enter the Brecksville Veterans Administration Hospital in Ohio, often considered one of the best gambling treatment programs. (Unfortunately, admission is limited to veterans.) According to Brenda:

■■■ *The Brecksville thing is pretty much standard addiction treatment, but it is geared towards compulsive gambling. And the people who run it are fantastic. They are very caring and they come as close, I think, to understanding the addiction of compulsive gambling as anybody who isn't a compulsive gambler can. And those are rare individuals. I had two [Twelve Step] meetings a week, but it's not the same as the [GA] Step meetings that got me going on working the Steps. But definitely, I had some in-depth exposure to the Steps, groups every morning, and I had to do an autobiography—oh dear, yes.* ■■■

Although inpatient treatment programs are focused on gambling problems, they deal with other issues as well. Typically, relationship problems are addressed, referrals are made to debt counselors, and mood disorders such as depression and anxiety are treated.

Outpatient Treatment

> "I just carried it all. I lived in the past, I lived in the future. I lived
> in guilt and shame about the past, and feared the future. I just
> couldn't live in the present moment." ▪▪▪ **Helen, age 61**

Of the women on the Internet survey who reported receiving
some kind of professional help, 36 specified outpatient counseling/
therapy, including outpatient treatment focused on gambling. Significantly, over one-fourth (29 percent) of the women who sought
professional help of any kind *did not mention their gambling problem* when they talked to their counselor; they focused on other life
problems. Why? Their reasons include shame or guilt, not understanding the nature and effects of compulsive gambling, and not
wanting to stop gambling, in spite of the problems. As Sarah put
it, "I was too ashamed and guilt-ridden to mention it. . . . I played
it off as depression."[14]

What did the women think of the outpatient professionals they
worked with? Responses ranged from "excellent" to "didn't know
what I was talking about." On the positive side, Clair described
the "wonderful" social worker she worked with for two months
as "her accountability." It was this counselor who introduced her
to Gamblers Anonymous. Mary sought out a psychologist because
of relationship issues with her husband, which surfaced after she
quit gambling. As she describes it:

> ▪▪▪ *I worked all day—it's a normal woman thing—I come home,
> he worked all day, he came home, his ass laid on the couch, I did
> the cooking and cleaning. Resentment. It seemed like I couldn't
> get over that hump. I was going to [GA] meetings, as many as I
> could, everything. But there was still something missing there. So
> I went to outside help, and that was one of the things that I talked
> about a lot. And [the counselor] kept saying, "What about Mary?"*

And anytime she would ask me that, my children came into the picture and my husband, but not me. And she said, "No, tell me about Mary." And I'm like, "Well . . ." and she'd say, "No, tell me about Mary." She was very helpful at making me see things that I never looked at that way before. Just little questions she would ask. ■■■

Sarah maintains that it is best to have the help of both GA and professional counselors. She says,

■■■ *Professional help helps you to get over the devastation of you going through shame, you going through guilt, you going through humiliation, you going through alienation from your family, your friends, and anybody that cares about you. If you are in bad enough shape to go to GA, then you are in bad enough shape that you have burnt a lot of bridges. GA can't help you build from square one like a professional could.* ■■■

Kay had been in recovery through GA for two years when she had the opportunity to join a women's professional counseling group. For her, participation in the group was invaluable:

■■■ *It has accelerated my recovery tremendously. I just don't know that I could have gotten everything that I have by just continuously working the GA Steps. I needed that professional guidance to bring those things out, give me permission, and give me assignments. It has really been helpful to me.* ■■■

While most of the women interviewed had positive results from outpatient professional help, others did not. Sometimes, this help was not successful because the woman was not ready to accept it. For example, Sharon describes going to a counselor who told her that she was profoundly depressed and she needed to go to GA. Sharon describes her response as "OK, thank you very much, have a nice day."

Most of the women who had negative experiences with professional help attribute this to the professionals' lack of knowledge about gambling problems. As Brenda puts it, "Someone who hasn't even grasped that an activity can be a dangerous addiction shouldn't be trying to treat compulsive gamblers." Sometimes, the advice of a counselor seemed useless to the study participants. Sophie's counselor told her to immediately call her father when she got an urge to gamble. But, according to Sophie, "That's sort of crazy, because if you got an urge to gamble you sure are not going to call your dad and tell him. He is always going to talk you out of it, so you are not going to call him in the first place!"

Other reasons given for not benefiting from counseling included comments such as "My doctor did not want to discuss it," and "I didn't want anyone to know how bad my gambling was." Those who were most satisfied worked with a professional who was trained to deal with gambling problems and/or who helped them find GA. Unfortunately, many professional counselors have no training on how to assess and treat compulsive gambling. Women in the Internet study encouraged professional helpers to become more aware of this potential problem and learn about GA resources in their community. Many women with gambling problems need professional help to discover more options. As Cindy said, "It is almost disgusting how hard someone needs to fall and how hard someone needs to do research in order to find help in this city. The problem exists for all different women in all walks of life, and it is as destructive as many other addictions."

Other thoughts from the women who sought help from professionals:

- "People that have screwed up their lives this bad, you know, need to be pointed in directions where people can help them, like consumer credit counseling."
- "[Counselors should] ask people questions, like, do you pay your bills on time, have you ever filed bankruptcy, do you have credit cards that are over their limit? How many credit cards do you have? Do you ever write hot checks? Do you take out loans? Do you owe your kids money? Are you in trouble financially?"
- "I think a person should be warned that when they stop one addiction, they usually go to another one. Nobody warned me in AA that I could get another addiction."
- "[My counselor] was really good about making me understand that it's a disease that can be treated through abstinence, but it's a cancer and if I keep feeding it, it can completely consume. She made me promise that I'm gonna go to those meetings, and to really try and share."

What kind of compassionate professional stance is helpful for such women? One anonymous counselor described it in the article "Reflections on Problem Gambling Therapy with Female Clients":[15]

> The women want good strategies from me, but this is not what I feel they demand most. They seem to want to know that I am there with them, to acknowledge that I see their pain and I am not afraid of them; that I can bear their stories and carry them, and that I will attend to them when they feel unworthy. I feel I am asked to testify to their survival; to help them see what I see: a person, deeply injured, and with great, unbelievable resilience.

Finding Effective Professional Help

Because the issue of problem gambling has not yet been consistently added to the training of helping professionals such as substance abuse counselors, social workers, psychologists, and physicians, there are many professionals who have never been exposed to the best treatment options for the problem. In some situations, the women in the Internet study found themselves teaching their counselor about the nature of problem gambling.

How can you find a professional who is already trained in this area? Look for one certified in counseling for gamblers. Certification means that at a minimum, counselors who are certified or licensed in a related field have attended training about the nature of problem gambling, how to assess severity, and how to put into practice a variety of methods that have been helpful to problem gamblers. Certification programs also require an internship with a professional who is already trained and practicing in the field. Most states have their own certification programs, and national certification is available through the National Council on Problem Gambling.

A quick way to locate certified counselors in your state is through the National Council on Problem Gambling Web site at www.ncpgambling.org. Click on the "Counselor" link to find a list of professionals. That Web site can also direct you to the toll-free number for your state's Council on Problem Gambling (available in most states), which can point you to certified counselors in your area. More and more states are funding problem gambling outpatient treatment, and a few, like Oregon, are also funding it on an inpatient basis. Your state Council on Problem Gambling can help you access such programs. Some Native American tribes have also set up counseling services, funded by the casino profits. Fortunately, these programs are either free or on a sliding scale.

As Lisa says, "By the time you have a gambling problem, you don't have the money to go to a professional. You have to depend on the state-funded mental health system or something on a sliding scale."

Although most of the women in the Internet survey benefited from the help of Gamblers Anonymous and/or professional help, a few were able to stop gambling "on their own" using a variety of strategies. The next chapter focuses on how they did it.

CHAPTER 8

Going It Alone

"No one really knows how to support and help you." ▪▪▪ **Jolene, age 56**

T he idea that "if you want something done, you better do it yourself" was passed down through the generations in my family. "Pulling yourself up by your own bootstraps" is almost a national anthem in the United States. The individualist ethic is everywhere in our culture. And, if you're a woman in trouble with compulsive gambling, add to the mix the shame, the guilt, and the limited treatment options, and it is not surprising that many women try to get free of the problem on their own.

Some of them succeed. According to a recent analysis of two representative national survey data, almost one-third of the people who had qualified as "pathological gamblers" according to *DSM-IV-TR* criteria experienced what is called "natural recovery."[1] In other words, they succeeded in quitting without professional treatment, without Gamblers Anonymous, and had no pathological gambling symptoms for at least a year. Only a very few of the participants with a history of gambling problems ever sought treatment or attended Gamblers Anonymous (7 percent in one study, 12 percent in the other).

Although the fact that many people recover from their addictions "naturally" is well supported and documented in addiction research, it is not commonly acknowledged by treatment providers working with substance abusers or compulsive gamblers. Some authors advocate for making fuller use of the strategies people use to successfully recover on their own.[2] In this chapter, we will focus on the successful strategies used by women whose road to recovery was the "natural" route.

Natural Recovery Strategies in Canada: A Study of Women in Ontario

In a 2002 study of 362 women with gambling problems in Ontario, only a small fraction (14 percent) had any experience with gambling treatment or Gamblers Anonymous.[3] Of the others, 40 percent reported they were successful in making changes on their own. "Making changes" included the goals of stopping gambling or gambling without the problems of spending too much money or time. Many women noted multiple strategies for coping with urges and meeting their goals. Listed in order of frequency, these included:

1. Willpower (90 percent)
2. Distracting themselves (87 percent)
3. Reminding themselves of the positive consequences of not gambling (82 percent)
4. Replacing gambling with other leisure activities (72 percent)
5. Reminding themselves of the problems created by gambling (71 percent)
6. Avoiding people and places that would trigger urges (62 percent)
7. Reducing access to money (54 percent)

As the authors of the study pointed out, it is interesting that reducing access to money, a common strategy of both gambling treatment and Gamblers Anonymous, is not a top strategy named by these women. Banning oneself from the casinos is not mentioned. It is also noteworthy that while the number-one strategy, "willpower," is compatible with a "pull yourself up by your bootstraps" philosophy, it is directly opposite GA's Step One: "We admitted we were powerless over gambling—that our lives had become unmanageable." Yet the women who were able to cope with their urges and maintain positive change used willpower as their primary strategy.

Natural Recovery Strategies in the U.S.: Women Surveyed in the Internet Study

In the Internet study, 10 percent of the women in recovery for six months or more had stopped gambling "on their own." When answering the GA Twenty Questions, these women reported significantly fewer symptoms than the group that received professional help or GA. They averaged sixteen "yes" answers, versus eighteen for the larger group, although both averages were well above the suggested cutoff score of seven.[4] This difference is noteworthy because it confirms other research that suggests people who recover on their own may be somewhat less seriously affected by the problem in the first place.

When asked to explain the "on their own" method, the women in the Internet survey reported many strategies:

1. Planning more activities to take the place of gambling.

   - "I found other things to do with myself . . . when I felt the urge to gamble, I'd go see a movie or treat myself in some other way."
   - "Started working more, joined social groups, told people about my problem."
   - "Made plans when the urge was not present. Like if the phone rang, I would make plans with a friend or make a commitment with someone that would prevent me from finding the time to go gambling."

2. Banning oneself from casinos.
   - "I had myself banned from the establishment where I gambled. I knew they would have me arrested if I set foot on the property. Thankfully, there is only one Indian casino here."
3. Moving out of the area where there are casinos.
   - "Moved to Tulsa, Oklahoma, where there are no video poker machines."
   - "Moved to another state where there is no gambling."
4. Summoning willpower.
   - "Mind over matter. Just took Prozac and made myself face the problem."
   - "Cold turkey. I decided that it's time for me to face the fact that gambling doesn't pay and I was wasting valuable time. When I would look around the casino I would see a lot of people I wouldn't want to associate with, and I realized that they may have looked like me at one time, but now they have deteriorated and that would happen to me."
5. Reviewing the negatives and the consequences of gambling.
   - "Told myself it was a waste of money."
   - "Remembering how badly I felt when I gamble, i.e., insomnia due to guilt, extreme anxiety."
   - "Deciding that the new business would never have a chance of surviving if I continued to gamble."
   - "Try to keep remembering all the harm it does."
   - "I understood what I am really risking! More than money."
6. Praying.
   - "Prayed for assistance and had no money."
7. Gaining support from others.
   - "Support from my husband."

These strategies are very similar to the ones reported by the Ontario women, with the addition of moving out of the area, and banning oneself from the casino. Moving out of the area away from casinos or video poker machines is commonly referred to as "the geographical cure" in Alcoholics Anonymous and other Twelve Step programs. It is generally agreed that it doesn't work, because "you bring yourself with you" to wherever you move. However, it does appear to help some people with compulsive gambling problems. Perhaps this is because when we take away the opportunity to gamble, cravings and urges to gamble greatly diminish. For those with alcohol problems, there is no practical way to totally avoid alcohol-buying opportunities in this culture—even in socalled dry counties, there is always a way to readily connect to a source. Unfortunately, with gambling now legal in every state but two, and new casinos being built every day, the days of isolating oneself from it may be limited.

Jolene's Strategy: "I Went Back into the Casino . . ."

Jolene, an Internet study participant, developed her own very unusual and finally successful method to stop the madness of her compulsive gambling after trying other more conventional ways that didn't help her. Strictly speaking, Jolene's situation doesn't quite fit the "on your own" category, because she was initially exposed to both counseling and GA. But they didn't work for her. She continued to gamble during and after each of these exposures. However, because her strategy was unique, it is worth a closer look.

Jolene attended GA for about a month, but was disappointed because "there were very few that had refrained from gambling for any long periods of time." She was in counseling with a psychologist for about six months "and it did nothing for me. Very pleasant person, I enjoyed visiting with him, but I felt I had a problem he couldn't address." She also tried hypnotism. After one three-hour session she stopped gambling for ten weeks, felt relaxed, felt good about herself, and then "I was totally shocked because I watched myself go right back to gambling."

By the time Jolene came up with her own strategy, she was in serious trouble. "I started staying out many nights. I had done that before, but not as extensively. It was getting to the point where I was a total disgrace to myself and my family and I didn't want to face them again and I felt it was just lies to say, 'I'll quit this time.' I was just totally exhausted, I didn't want to think about it, and I didn't want to cope with it."

In her despair, an idea came to her as she woke up one morning. She thought, "I have to do this, because if I don't get this resolved, I might as well be a street person." Jolene set about directly observing the consequences of gambling on fellow casino-goers over a period of four and a half weeks. Prompted by this flood of information, she was able to rethink the meaning of gambling. This summary of her project is taken from her own words.

■■■ *I got up in the morning and I packed a little bag, and I told my adult children, "I'm going to the casino and I'm staying until I resolve the problem. I'm going as an observer, I don't have any money. I'm not borrowing any money, either. But I'm not returning if I can't come back and regain a fairly decent life, where I have goals and dreams to look forward to."*

I parked fairly close to the casino where I thought the lighting was good. I didn't know what I was going to do from day to day. I didn't know how I was going to eat or anything, but I knew I had to find an answer for myself. When I went in the casino I had several notebooks with me. I first visited with friends I had known for many years, and I told them, "Here's the reason I'm here, nope, I'm not gambling. I'm just going to observe, and if you'd like to talk to me, I'm available," because they knew I was a gambler too. I told them I was going to write a book, and I want to create an awareness that there are ways of resolving this thing, and for those who haven't yet gambled maybe it will make them realize that it's not the thing to do.

Everybody talked to me, even total strangers. I probably talked to 350 or 400 people in the four and a half weeks I was there. I never asked a question. I just listened. I didn't want to gamble because I had a mission. I wanted to find out why we gamble, why I gamble, and what was controlling me. I talked to a lot of people in their last stage of gambling. One man, I spent two or three days with him. He was seventy-one years old and he didn't feel there was any hope for him. He gambled five to seven days a week. Literally hated himself for it. The young married people in their mid-twenties and thirties were scared out of their minds because they were so discouraged. Everyone asked me the question, "Why do we do it?"

I wrote notes, and each day I would review my notes and think about myself and my reactions to what I had written down. For some reason, no one at the casino caught me. I would clean up in the bathroom, sleep in the car, and about once a week I'd come home and do my laundry when no one was at home. One evening when I reviewed my notes, I said to myself, "I know what happens, I know what happens to gamblers, and I know how to take care of it for myself." The next morning I left, and that was it. I left with the greatest peace of mind, no torment of any kind. My family says that my presence and the look on my face, the way I moved and acted, told them I was not going to gamble again. ▪▪▪

Through the process of talking to many gamblers experiencing heavy consequences for their gambling, Jolene developed a change plan that enabled her to stop. For her, this involved merging the various contrary files in her head about gambling. On the one hand, the "winning file had all the great things about gambling."

This included not just the wins, but the unique atmosphere of casinos, where the lights are dim, the machines tinkle, and time is not important. On the other hand, Jolene feels that her conscious mind kept a good record of all the bad consequences from gambling, and "all the crap I went through." By flooding her mind with actual observations of what was happening to other gamblers, Jolene felt she could "bring the two files together." Merging the files "did away with all the wonderful things in the winning file." She is now able to see that her "winning file is a false illusion, it's a fantasy land, a fantasy world, it's dangerous."

Although Jolene's process is somewhat simplified here, the basic idea is consistent with the cognitive-behavioral principles outlined in chapter 7. How you think about your gambling experience influences your gambling behavior. In Jolene's situation, she found freedom from gambling by forcing herself to take a good, long, hard look at what *really* happens—not the fantasy thoughts of winning, relaxing, a few minutes of entertainment or relief from mounting stress. Finding a way to look and stay looking at reality, not wishful thinking, seems to be the key to long-term recovery for many compulsive gamblers. Some women can find this by regularly attending GA and listening to the experiences of fellow gamblers. Others finally focus on reality with the help of professionals. For Jolene, it took four and a half solid weeks of listening to what was happening in the casino to her fellow gamblers.

Cautions about "Going It Alone"

Children are good at asking for help at the first sign of distress. They usually don't attempt to bandage their own knees or comfort themselves when they have nightmares. However, as we become adults, this natural ability to ask for help from others seems to disappear. We think we have to do it all ourselves. Most women who begin to realize that their gambling is much more intense than that of their friends, or causes too many fights with their spouse or partner, or makes bill-paying impossible, start trying home remedies.

Home remedies, such as willpower, distraction, prayer, and firm self-reminders of the consequences, can sometimes work just fine, according to the research. Self-help manuals using the cognitive-behavioral approach have been found to be helpful to those working on their own.[5] Sometimes, a person can stop gambling altogether or even learn to gamble without experiencing negative consequences.

However, most of the women in the Internet survey tried home remedies (over and over again) without success. No matter how many times they left their credit cards at home to limit their gambling at the casino, they ended up driving back to get them. No matter how many times they willed themselves to never go back, they did. That's why the majority of the women (90 percent) finally resorted to asking for help, either from GA, professionals, or both. As noted in chapter 4, many of these women were in desperate condition before they could ask for help.

The caution raised here is: *Don't wait too long.* If the strategies for self-help are not working for you, you don't have to suffer alone. Continuing to suffer alone and gamble compulsively can lead to long-term financial ruin, prison, homelessness, severed relationships, and suicide. Many women have experienced great relief by confiding in another person the true nature of their gambling problem, and asking that person to help them find help. It's the first step of finally taking your life back from compulsive gambling, when your own efforts to stop aren't working. *Don't wait too long.*

CHAPTER 9

Families and Friends— Healing Relationships

"He was, like, 'What's going to make it work this time?' "

▪▪▪ **Eva, age 46**

Deep in our hearts, most of us wish to be cuddled and protected by a loving family when times are rough. But even when a family has such a capacity to love and protect, compulsive gambling is likely to at least temporarily destroy it. There is something about a woman gambling away the family nest egg, pawning the wedding rings, or maxing out credit cards that becomes unforgivable in the eyes of many husbands and partners. The fact that recovery from compulsive gambling usually involves relapses can make family members and friends wary of reengagement. As Eva says about her husband's reaction to another relapse and promise to quit, "He was, like, 'What's going to make it work this time?'"

One of the few research studies on families of women gamblers confirms that pathological gambling significantly disrupts family relationships, and that they are more conflict-oriented and disorganized than families who don't have this problem.[1] Susan explains how her gambling affected her daughter:

■■■ *I used to pawn everything we owned, you know, come home and tell her I am sorry, I am never going to do it again. And I would go to GA meetings and she would go to Gam-Anon, and I would gamble again. I mean the poor kid lost her childhood. Her whole high school years were spent taking care of me.* ■■■

The pain and suffering inflicted on family members are among the biggest regrets reported by the women in the Internet study. When asked "What do you regret the very most when you look back over your compulsive gambling days?" many respondents gave answers that were about family members:

■ "The utter look of betrayal from my one and only true friend, my husband."
■ "All the lying to friends, family, and myself."
■ "Robbing the family of time, love, and for not being there."
■ "The loss of income and time with my family."
■ "Hurting my husband, and the lies that I have told him regarding money."
■ "The huge financial pressure I put on my husband, causing him to overwork."

Dealing with the regrets around family and friends is one of the most important and difficult challenges in maintaining recovery. It can be done, but in the early stages of recovery it takes ongoing vigilance to avoid slipping into a morass of guilt and remorse. In this chapter, we will look at several issues concerning families and friends, specifically:

■ how relationships get broken
■ how family and friends can support the recovering gambler
■ how you can help friends and family
■ how to cope with the guilt over the harm your gambling has done to the family (especially children)

- how the family picture changes when you stop gambling destructively

Broken Relationships

The woman who stops gambling compulsively is immediately faced with what is called in Alcoholics Anonymous "the wreckage of the past." Broken relationships are common. Usually family and friends have initiated the break, but sometimes the woman herself cuts off a relationship in order to support her own recovery.

It is pretty easy to understand why family and friends may want to distance themselves. When a person crosses the line into gambling compulsively, values previously held dear seem to slip away. Behaviors that would never have occurred in the past, such as lying to family members and friends, become automatic. Jodi explains how she did this more and more often with her husband, until she got caught:

> ▪▪▪ *I was trying to hide it, so I would sneak gambling when he was at work or at school. I would go when I knew I had an opportunity to go and I wouldn't be confronted about it. Since John was always working, I just said, "Oh, I'll be working late." But we all know that we stay longer than we had planned, so we get caught.* ▪▪▪

Seeing a pattern of unexplained absences and continuous excuses, some spouses and partners concluded that their mate was having an extramarital affair. In a way, she was, only the object of her affection was not a person but gambling.

Family members who are directly affected by the consequences of compulsive gambling tend to feel deeply hurt and angry when they finally understand the extent of the damage and deception. It is hard to become supportive in such a state. At the same time, the gambler is feeling depressed, demoralized, desperate, and fearful of losing these important relationships. Consequently, not all families survive. Lisa has had to accept the fact that some of her meaningful relationships have been broken beyond repair. Compared to her husband's ongoing alcoholism for the twenty-five years of their marriage, the effects of her gambling came on swiftly and hit deep. As she describes it:

> ▪▪▪ My husband can continue on with his addiction to alcohol. It's not doing him any good, but it hasn't devastated our family. My two and a half years of gambling totally wiped out my family. I think the quickness of gambling and how much it destroys families is a lot faster than any other addiction or compulsion that's around. Some people I have lost permanently. I have to accept that I'm never going to have them in my life again. I've lost them through their attitude of "How could you do that?" and they are forever out of my life. I can't undo a single thing I did to anybody, [I can only] apologize and try to make amends to them financially. I have to keep reminding myself that the past is the past. ▪▪▪

Accepting the kinds of losses that one cannot change is one of the most intense ongoing challenges to the process of recovery. This is often especially difficult for women because of the importance relationships and connection play in their lives.

However, sometimes a woman has to break important relationships herself in order to support her own recovery. Irene found that she had to stop seeing the friend of ten years who gambled along with her and was still gambling. "It was a horrible thing," she says. "I told her I can't see her anymore because every time I look at you or I am with you, you remind me of gambling. I just told her I couldn't see her anymore and continue to stay clean. She understood. I tried to talk her into going to GA, but it didn't work."

In Sarah's case, she came to the point of threatening to divorce her husband in order to resume her participation in GA. After two and a half years of regular GA attendance and no gambling, she gave in to the pressure from her husband to quit going to meetings. Her husband resented the time she spent there and, as she says, "I had to fight for every meeting." After another two and a half years, she had a major relapse and went back to GA with renewed determination.

■■■ *After that first meeting, I went back home that night and looked George square in the eye. I said, "I'm going to tell you this, and I'm only going to tell you this one time. I will never give up my recovery for you, for my kids, or a house, or my job, or anything." I said, "This is my life. Mine, not yours, that we're talking about. I gave it up once and I'm not willing to give it up a second time. So if you are not comfortable with that or can't handle that, you need to go now. Because that's the way it's going to be, and I'm not going to allow you to interfere with this anymore."* ■■■

Putting her recovery first, above everything else in her life, was new to Sarah. As it turned out, taking this stance worked for her and her husband. He became willing to deal with his own anxiety issues and she was able to focus on recovery through GA.

When one of the issues a person may be trying to escape through gambling is a dysfunctional marriage or relationship, quitting can bring things to a head. A spouse or partner can react to the deception and financial ruin as the last straw in a fragile relationship. And a guilt-ridden gambler who has been trying to placate her partner may finally find her own voice. As Terri describes it:

■■■ *Our marriage was not real good anyway at that point, and when he realized all the lies that I told and everything I'd done, it really hurt him. He was not a violent person, he was just deeply hurt. And of course, there was a lot of trust gone. But on the other hand, there was a lot of resentment and anger on my part, too, toward him. I started venting that. It really started coming out after I stopped gambling.* ▪ ▪ ▪

Another woman wrote about how difficult it was to come back into the reality of her marriage without the escape that gambling had provided. She said, "It was like bringing a camera lens back into focus. The ugly part of your life never really went away and you still have to deal with it."

Some of these broken relationships were mended in recovery, but some weren't. Families can cause great pain, but sometimes family members can be helpful to a woman's recovery.

How Families and Friends Can Help

Family members and friends have the potential to be a blessing to a woman in trouble with gambling. In addition to love and compassion, they can provide concrete support in terms of accountability, money management, and activities to fill the void of not gambling. Women in the Internet study listed these comments among the many ways they felt support from their families and friends:

- "Tough love."
- "The message board contacts [from an Internet forum] provided a safe place to express my feelings and share my story. I felt accepted and loved by almost every person who posted there, and part of a group struggling to come to terms with what we had done to ourselves and our significant others."
- "Understanding and patience."
- "I have become closer with my family. I feel loved."
- "Being there when needed."
- "Understanding, comfort, strength and acceptance."

- "My family being there with me when I went to town, the danger area."
- "Offering help to help me stop and taking charge of the credit cards and bank accounts."

Having a partner or friend take over your finances in the early stages of recovery can be a tremendous relief, even if you don't like "losing your independence." Joanne had her younger sister regularly review her payable bills, which kept her from taking out money for gambling. "I don't like having to do that," she says, "being forty-one years old and having my twenty-three-year-old sister look at my bankbook. But it's what I have to do right now."

Families and friends can also be a resource to fill the hole that was previously taken up by frequent gambling. Reclaiming family activities that you used to enjoy, or deliberately scheduling get-togethers with friends who you haven't seen in a while, can help fill the great void that develops. For people who have no family nearby, or who are isolated because of their gambling, other activities can help. Irene was sixty-five when she first started going to GA. People in the program kept telling her that she needed to find something other than gambling to get interested in, such as finding a job. But Irene hadn't worked since 1983, was disabled, divorced, and had no family living in her area. Instead, she learned to "fill the hole" in other ways: she read a lot, went back to church, learned to use a computer, volunteered for the board of her housing authority, and became the treasurer of the GA group.

Families can also convey to a woman that she is much more than just a problem gambler. She has many important roles: mother, grandmother, wife, partner, community member, employee. Family members and friends can help her regain her confidence in functioning in these roles. After Jessie got out of prison for her embezzling crime, she found strength to pick up the pieces of her life through the support of her children and grandchildren. She explains, "I think the most supporting thing was that my kids love me and my grandchildren love me. My grandchildren are very precious to me, and because they still loved me it made me feel like I was OK. I was a good grandmother and I could be a good grandmother for as long as I live. And that meant a lot to me. Just having the love of my family."

When the women of the Internet survey were asked to indicate the most important support systems to them in their recovery (they could choose more than one), 40 percent said their friends, 36 percent said a spouse or partner, 29 percent said children, and 18 percent said parents. Clearly, families and friends can provide much needed support. Still, 70 percent of the women identified Gamblers Anonymous members as their most important means of support.[2]

GA members may offer the most support because they can provide two things that are initially difficult for families and friends: first, immediate acceptance of the compulsive gambler, no matter what she has done to sustain her gambling; and second, the knowledge and understanding of how compulsive gambling takes over a person's life. If families and friends could become more knowledgeable about compulsive gambling, they might be able to offer more support. Let's look at some concrete things recovering women can do to help family members and friends become more informed.

Helping Families Understand the Problem

Compulsive gambling is known as the "hidden addiction" for a reason. Not only is it easy to hide (up to a point) from family members, friends, and employers, it is also still hidden as a problem from the general public. Many people view gambling as merely "gaming," an activity that helps prop up state budgets, so it can't be so bad, they think. It just doesn't make much sense to the general public that a casual behavior choice for most people can become a compulsion that wreaks havoc on individuals and their families. After all, no outside agent such as drugs or alcohol is put into a person's body. "Why can't she just quit?" is an often-heard complaint. Families and friends mirror these general attitudes, which are common in our culture. Until recently, even professionals in the addiction field had little or no comprehension of the problem, nor did they offer much help. Women who themselves are caught in the cycle of compulsive gambling can't understand their own behaviors, and sometimes think they must be "going crazy." Given the uninformed state of almost everyone about compulsive gambling, it is no wonder that many women are blamed and rejected for their gambling problems without further investigation.

There are several ways to help family members and friends learn more about compulsive gambling, including literature, Gam-Anon and Gamblers Anonymous meetings, family treatment groups, and counseling.

Literature

Share some good reading material. When you finish reading this book, ask someone close to you to read it: your spouse, partner, friend, or adult child, for example. Visit the National Council on Problem Gambling Web site at www.ncpgambling.org and order any or all of the reasonably priced pamphlets (one to four dollars), such as *Understanding Compulsive Gambling* or *When Someone You Love Gambles*. An excellent free resource is the www.problem gambling.ca Web site, developed by the Centre for Addiction and Mental Health in Toronto. It has a wealth of information and research, and an especially informative section for families under the "Getting Help" link. Many state Helplines offer free materials for compulsive gamblers and their families. You can usually find your own state gambling Helpline in the local Yellow Pages, or go to the National Council on Problem Gambling site online. The Gam-Anon Web site at www.gam-anon.org offers information about this organization for friends and family, and targeted information for people who are living with a compulsive gambler. Finally, the resource section of this book lists several other resources.

Gam-Anon Meetings

The purpose of Gam-Anon, in its words, is to help people in relationships with compulsive gamblers resolve "the problems you are facing in your life due to the gambling problem."[3] One of the benefits for compulsive gamblers is that the family member is encouraged to work on his or her own problems and develop coping strategies, instead of trying to control the gambler. As Sandy discovered, this can be a welcome relief. She says of her husband, "Until Paul went to Gam-Anon, he just viewed the situation as 'you get better or else.' Now that he's started going to Gam-Anon, he's starting to get more of a grip that there are really things about him that need to change. That's been good."

Open Gamblers Anonymous Meetings

Sandy has also taken her daughter and her husband to several GA meetings that are open to families and friends as well. She says this has helped a great deal in decreasing the amount of negative judgment they have toward her. According to Sandy, "They get to see more of the illness and what the illness does. I know it doesn't change their pain or their hurt or their being betrayed or any of that, but it helps them understand that it's not necessarily me that wanted to treat them that way. It was the disease talking." Be sure to check your local GA schedule for open meetings (see www.gamblersanonymous.org), as many meetings are "closed," meaning they are for gamblers only. If the type of meeting is not specified in the schedule, assume it is a closed meeting.

Family Treatment Groups and Professional Counseling

Alcohol and drug treatment programs have long recognized that "addiction is a family disease" and have provided therapeutic help to families affected by members with drug or alcohol problems. Many gambling treatment programs have followed that lead, offering weekly family groups and/or individual counseling to family members as part of the treatment package. If you plan to participate in a gambling treatment program, investigate the possibility of including your family in some way.

Jennifer was working with a professional counselor who was knowledgeable about gambling. After a relapse, her marital problems got immediately worse. She describes her situation:

■■■ *There was jealousy about going to the GA meetings, and he was real smothering, wanting to make sure where I was all the time. I had no freedom. He was very, very upset—not so much [about] the money, but all the lying that went on. And the fear of losing me. He thought I was going to come through recovery and then leave. It was scary because I had no safety at home. I was always scared about saying something because I wasn't sure of his reaction. I'm not saying I wasn't a schmuck for what I did. But nobody needs to be treated like that day in and day out when you're trying to work a program and you are being honest and upfront.* ■■■

When her husband got involved with her in professional counseling, her home environment began to improve. In addition, Jennifer brought her husband to a few open GA meetings and introduced him to the wife of another recovering gambler, so that he would have someone who understood his situation. The counseling format gave them both a sense of safety, a place where they could talk honestly about the issues in their relationship. She concludes:

> ▪▪▪ *It really did help, it did. The counseling, balanced with church, made him willing to give a little bit more. There was some bruising and tenderness there. He was still pretty tender over what I had done, and because I hadn't come clean, he was still always trying to dig for the truth. The counselor allowed us a place to have safety and also made me accountable. I'd say it took a good six months to get through that relapse.* ▪▪▪

But in some situations the spouse or partner or friend doesn't want to learn anything about compulsive gambling, period. With such people, this may happen when they themselves are engaging in problem gambling. They are likely to feel threatened by a gambling partner who suddenly takes a different path. One woman in the Internet survey wrote that her spouse still gambles, and "recovery seems to threaten our relationship. Admitting my addiction to my spouse made us further apart." As in the case of Irene, who cut off her relationship with her friend of ten years, action may be called for to protect your own recovery.

Helping loved ones get more information about problem gambling through literature, meetings, or professional counseling opens channels to communicate about some behaviors and consequences that may otherwise be very difficult to talk about. As family members learn more about compulsive gambling, your behaviors will no longer seem unique. They may begin to see your actions as part of the typical pattern of a compulsive gambler, instead of a deliberate plot to terrify and hurt them. As Sandy says, it doesn't change their hurt and pain, but it does offer a bridge to communication and understanding.

Restoring Trust and "Screaming the Serenity Prayer"

In the long run, the only way to restore trust with family members may be to take responsibility for your current behavior, stop lying about your gambling, stop putting the family in financial jeopardy because of your gambling, stop absenting yourself from the family to gamble—that is, *stop gambling*. Even then, because of the typical pattern of broken promises and not telling the truth while you were gambling, restoring trust with family members and friends can take months and sometimes years. As Jan explains, the process of rebuilding and healing relationships is not easy:

> ▪▪▪ *I paid back the money to my family, and took a long time doing it. And then my husband and I have so much that we've done to each other, with his drinking and my gambling, that really the only amends that we've ever done . . . is to just keep living and to try and do it. It doesn't mean that it's been easy. I can remember screaming the Serenity Prayer at him and him screaming it back . . . [and asking,] "Isn't it time you called your sponsor?!!" So I can't say it's easy.* ▪▪▪

Sometimes, making a commitment to consistently do things that put barriers between you and gambling helps to restore trust. For Susan, accepting her own limitations about managing money led her to make a long-term commitment for herself to not go anywhere outside her home on her own and to carry only limited cash. Her immediate family supports her in this by going with her on errands. "My husband and I do the grocery shopping together," she says. "If I need clothes, I take my daughter or my husband, or if they need something we go together." At the time of the interview, she had been doing this for eighteen months. Other women who were interviewed made a commitment for themselves to go to ninety GA meetings in ninety days—and did it. These kinds of actions, when followed through on, can reassure family members that you are indeed serious about quitting gambling and that you can make commitments and keep them. However, it is important to note that these commitments were not imposed by family members, but came from the women themselves.

The Special Issue of Children

It is very painful to become aware of how compulsive gambling has affected your children. When asked, "What do you regret the most when you look back over your days of compulsive gambling?" many of the women in the Internet study responded with regrets about the consequences their children experienced. For example:

- "The pain and distrust it caused in my children's eyes."
- "Time away from the children and losing their college money."
- "Loss of valuable time with my children."
- "Losing my children as friends."
- "Missed important events in my children's lives."
- "The times I left my children in situations that in hindsight were completely dangerous. Times I could have spent with them. These days I cannot retrieve."

The hard truth is that there is no way to do it over. The women who are maintaining their recovery and have such deep regrets about their family, and especially their children, are learning how to live with that truth. The Twelve Step mantra "One day at a time" is part of the process of restoring one's dignity and self-respect in spite of past mistakes. The Serenity Prayer helps. Clara says, "Just be gentle on yourself right now. Don't go into the 'I'm terrible' place. Just try to be gentle and keep making the right decisions, right now."

Serenity Prayer

God, grant me the serenity
To accept the things I cannot change,
The courage to change the things I can,
And the wisdom to know the difference.

The question of how much to tell the children about your gambling may become an issue in recovery. Sometimes it's just obvious, because the children are still living at home, but are old enough to notice what's happening with their mom and how it's affecting them. At fifteen, Katy's oldest daughter knew the extent of her gambling and was even involved with the treatment program's family recovery. However, her eight- and ten-year-old children did not know about her gambling. Tina did not tell her adult children for about a year after she quit gambling, and even then, did not tell them how bad her situation had become. However, she says, "If I saw them heading in that same direction, I would definitely step in and tell them every gory detail. But right now, I just don't see the need for it. And they don't understand it, so it's just not necessary."

Children can be both supportive and angry when they find out the truth about your gambling. Katy describes her fifteen-year-old daughter as "supportive, but she was mad too." Lisa's children were "glad they had their mom back," but "They would also throw things up to me every once in a while about 'Gee, we could have had this if you didn't gamble all our money away.'"

The children's anger can hook into a mother's guilt about the mistakes she made. Lisa feels particularly bad about leaving her older daughter in charge of her younger son, and missing her daughter's sixteenth birthday. She says, "I really didn't know much about her last two years of school and she probably really needed me from the time she was sixteen to eighteen, and I just wasn't around that much." She attributes the fact that they are honor students and wonderful kids to "God guiding them and taking care of them while my husband and I were too immature to take care of our own children." In her two years of recovery, she has been "doing my darnedest to be responsible in everything and taking care of every obligation that I need to take care of."

How Recovery Changes the Family Picture

In spite of all their mistakes with family members and friends, the women in the Internet survey found a new life when they quit gambling, especially concerning their relationships. They no longer felt isolated from family, children, and friends, since they were no longer lying to them. They could resume their cultural roles of caretaking and relationship tending. In recovery, the women were most proud and satisfied about developments like these:

- "Created more love in my life."
- "No lies, self-esteem coming back."
- "Feeling good about me, [and having] my children's trust again."
- "I have myself back."
- "Positive contributing member to my family and community."
- "I can help others."
- "Children are happier."
- "More time to spend with my family."
- "The friends I've made and the love and trust of my children."

Ariel's experience illustrates how the skills learned in recovery can help a person deal with the bumps and bruises of family life that continue long after a person stops gambling. After many relapses, Ariel's continuous recovery started after she was picked up for a DUI and ordered to alcohol/drug treatment. Here is her story:

▪▪▪ *Before gambling took hold of me, I would describe myself as a generally successful entrepreneur who was in the midst of recreating my career after the experience of a failed business. Finances were tight. I have three grown children, one of whom is home every other week, and lived with my second husband. I must have been drinking more than I thought, because in March 2000, I had a scare with my liver and became jaundiced. Luckily it was not permanently damaged, but I quit drinking. It was difficult, but I did it myself and did not go through any program.*

During this period I had a job as an outside salesperson, with my office at home and my own hours. Some of my clients were located near the newly built casino, which was about twenty minutes from my home. I think a combination of several things (stopping drinking, nearness of the casino, time on my hands) made going to the casino very attractive. I would stop in occasionally and spend twenty or thirty dollars and go home. I started going more frequently, and one day I won a $1,500 jackpot. This was the only time that I told my husband and friends that I had won something at the casino. I remember him telling me to take the money and spend it on whatever I wanted, even though we were struggling financially. I think I spent all of it back at the casino and started to plan my day around getting out there. I would make sure that I got home to make dinner for my husband or pick up my son from school.

I continued gambling, hiding it, and spent the daily maximum amount of money I could get on our debit card. I did not have access to credit cards, due to some business losses. A few months after I started hiding my gambling, I got caught. My husband came home with a used car that he really wanted to get, and he thought we had five thousand dollars in our account. I had to tell him that we did not have any money in the account. He was shocked when I told him what I had been doing. He told me that it was OK and that if I stopped now, everything would be OK. I said I would, and meant every word.

However, by October of that year I was back to secretly gambling. At some point my husband caught on again and told me I had to seek help. I called GA and went to my first meeting. I was scared, but it was OK, and I tried to go to meetings a couple of times a week. One of the things I learned in GA was how to get more money for gambling. I actually had not thought about payday loans or pawning anything to get money until I heard about it in GA. So I pawned my husband's digital camera, guitar, amplifier, his mother's wedding ring, and so on. I also started to get into the payday loan cycle, which was a nightmare.

In January 2001, my husband took away my checkbook and debit card and took my name off the account. I had periods of abstinence and relapse and then decided to enter an outpatient program for gambling sponsored by the state. It was group therapy with additional individual sessions. I managed to get six months of abstinence—the most I had ever had since starting gambling. Unfortunately, the state funding ran out and the program was closed. During that time I continued to go to GA and also remained abstinent from alcohol. Although this is no excuse, without the program, some of us saw a green light and went back out.

During the next year and half, I continued to gamble and took up drinking again. My husband continued working and I got another job with regular hours. We sold our property and home (it was commercial) and had some extra cash in the bank. When I drank, it really made me want to gamble. I lied about everything, stole checks, stole money from my hospitalized mother-in-law, stole money from my friend's purses, pawned my wedding ring, had eight payday loans going at one time. My teenage son was still with us every other week and he was heading in the wrong direction, drinking, smoking pot, and I was not around very much. Most of my *time at work was spent figuring out how I was going to pay my bills and payday loans and have money to gamble. It was a nightmare.*

By July of 2003, my husband had just about had it. He found all the stolen checks I had taken and written to the casino. He told me that he might as well not even work because I just gambled it away. He went to an attorney and had separation papers drawn up and gave them to me. My husband decided to leave the area and find work as a way to see if that would help me figure out what I was going to do about my problem. He went to Las Vegas. I was sad but thought it would be great to do whatever I wanted to do without anyone telling me whether I could drink or gamble. I proceeded to dig myself into a very big hole and got to the point, by February 2004, of having nothing and being unable to pay rent, have money for groceries, and so on. My husband was sending me money from Vegas to pay the rent, and you know where that went. I got a second job typing up policies for a hospital and I charged them almost double what it actually took me to do the job, to finance my gambling.

My husband has his own issues and he was unable to make it in Vegas, and he returned home in March of that year. He was mentally spent and so was I. We decided to live together and work on ourselves independently and see how it ended up. He would not bother me about what I did, and I would not bother him. We would just try to survive and see what happened. I went back to GA and he started looking for a job. He found a job working nights. I went out to the casino when he left for work and got home about four a.m. and went to work at eight a.m.

On May 22 I gave a party for my girlfriend to celebrate her new house. It lasted all afternoon and after everyone left I proceeded to get in my car and head to the casino. I was very drunk and was pulled over and booked for a DUI. It was horrible, and I ended up going into a deferred program with intensive outpatient treatment (three hours, four nights a week) with two or three mandatory GA or AA meetings a week. I addition, I was involved in starting a GA women's group on Thursday nights to work the Steps.

The women's group meeting was pivotal to my recovery. We decided to sponsor each other, since there were no women in the program with any clean time. We wrote out and shared our work on the Steps, honestly and heartfelt. We laughed, we cried, we had coffee and made plans to help each other when a vulnerable time was coming up, tempting us to gamble. We went to movies, made dream boards [collages of pictures that symbolized the future we hoped for], river rafted, went to church, trying to fill up the time we used to spend gambling. Going through the Fourth and Fifth Steps was a breakthrough for me with this group. I pulled away the layers and character defects that I had been living with forever. With the alcohol treatment program, I was doing something for my recovery almost every day of the week. I began to be able to look in the mirror and not feel guilty. I also rescued a ten-year-old bison frise named Scooter that I always called my "recovery dog." He was something to take care of and be with me in the car so I would not gamble. I also took up knitting those frilly scarves and managed to compulsively knit one for everyone I knew (thirty-five of them). My life is so full now that I don't know where the time would be to gamble. It was important to find positive things to fill up our void.

This was a very intensive time for me. The combination of hours of treatment and working the Steps kept me abstinent till now, which is four years, three months. I continue to work the GA program, go to meetings, and also be of service to our group by opening meetings and being a board member. I believe it takes a combination of things to click our brain into recovery mode. The hard part is that it is different for every single person. Having a husband who loves and supports me has been critical, as well as the GA program. I don't know how it would have turned out if I was single, and I don't want to know.

My life slowly began to turn around financially and spiritually. My relationships got better; my job blossomed. I have made several friends in this program and owe much of my success to this. I am involved with GA to remind myself of the awful painful times that I could return to in an instant, with one bet.

Life does not stop or become serene just because I'm not gambling. I have had some real challenges while maintaining my abstinence. My youngest son has been battling his addiction to cocaine, OxyContin, and alcohol. He was in jail and now faces prison for at least one year. During this time I also broke my ankle and had to have surgery. My husband had a big fight with my grown daughter and they are on the outs. I have a new granddaughter, and my son is not married to her mother and things are very tense. I am also having stress in my job, which I have not had for a long time, and I am the sole financial support of my family. I am staying calm and trying to be focused and have faith that it will work out. I really thought about gambling during all these crises, but did not. I kept in touch with everyone and went to meetings. I also went to a counselor every week during this time, which helped.

Getting through these times and learning how to get through them without escaping to a slot machine is my everyday goal. I have become a more patient person, and I try to live the Serenity Prayer every day. It is so hard when you want to help your child get better and you cannot. In the old days I would have felt like running away. I don't today. I stand up to my problems and work through them.

What can I say? If it weren't for the GA program and recovering gambler friends, I don't know if I could have made it this long. I also stay away from any gambling, which is hard when most of the entertainment in this town is at the casino, along with two high school reunions that I did not attend. I have a regional meeting *for my work next January that I really enjoy but will not be attending because it is in Reno. I am smart enough to know that I would defi-nitely gamble if placed in that venue. My plan is to not gamble today, and that is all I really have. I have a connection in my head, thank God, that sitting at a slot machine equals loss of self and my life. I will be in this program the rest of my life.* ■ ■ ■

For Ariel and the other women in the Internet survey, the struggle to quit gambling was well worth it, especially in regard to the health of their relationships. In chapter 10 we'll learn more about how they maintained their recovery over the long term, and what the meaning of recovery came to be for them as they picked up the pieces of their lives.

CHAPTER 10

Maintaining Recovery

"I just look at this whole thing like, when you walk up a down escalator. You can do it, but if you stop, you immediately start going down. You can't hang out; you can't think you've got it made."
■■■ **Brenda, age 46**

The maintenance stage of any kind of change is always the hardest. To reword a famous quote often attributed to Mark Twain, "It's easy to quit gambling . . . I've done it hundreds of times." One of the greatest threats to maintaining recovery is to become complacent, or "think you've got it made." In this chapter we will explore how the women in the Internet study maintained their vigilance over their recovery, months and years after stopping gambling, and we'll look at some tips on how you can maintain your own recovery.

Their recovery recipe, in general, consists of three parts: (1) guarding themselves from relapsing into gambling by taking protective measures, (2) developing a realistic plan for how to stop a relapse if one should occur and get back to recovery, and (3) gathering their strength and reaching out to learn new coping skills and new ways to reward themselves. As they progressed on this journey, the meaning of recovery in their own lives became clearer and more precious to them.

The Good News about Recovery: "There's a Woodpecker Outside My Door"

In contrast to gambling itself, meaningful payoffs keep on coming and coming after one stops compulsive gambling. Although each woman experiences her own unique rewards, some common themes were reported by the women in the Internet survey. Improved emotional well-being (90 percent) and the relief from no longer lying (86 percent) were checked as the top two benefits for most of the women. Other significant benefits chosen were relief from depression (49 percent), resuming church or spiritual practices (45 percent), regaining relationships with friends (43 percent) and children (41 percent), and restoration of physical health (also 41 percent). The two items on the survey that related to improving finances were not selected among the top benefits.[1] The fact that this area was not as important as improving one's emotional well-being and no longer lying suggests a lot about the importance of emotional stability to the respondents.

Another question on the Internet survey was "What has been the most satisfying part of the recovery process for you?" Answers reveal a range of important benefits: some satisfactions that had been lost to compulsive gambling, and some that were new, never experienced by the woman until her recovery. For example:

- "Being able to stay away for almost four years now, having my own apartment, no debt, and emotional freedom."
- "To be involved in a program that allows me the privilege of helping other compulsive gamblers."
- "The return to being honest."
- "Loving life again."
- "Spiritual awareness."
- "Regaining my self-respect."
- "My life is less of a mess than when I was gambling."

- "Life can be stressful sometimes, but I can now deal with the stress by going to GA and not to the casinos."
- "Knowing that I can sleep at night, not having to worry about yesterday or tomorrow."
- "I see myself no longer on the survival slope of life. I am beginning to grow, learn, and achieve. Retaining my recovery has rewards, not consequences."
- "Saving hard-earned money."
- "Having my family back and getting peace and freedom within my own person."
- "I am now going back to school to become an addiction counselor. I feel a strong desire to 'give back' and help others who are suffering."
- "Knowing that there is a light at the end of the tunnel."
- "Getting up in the morning and looking in the mirror at this person and being able to say, 'I like you.'"

Some of these statements reflect a renewed sense of awe and wonder about life, as though the women had narrowly escaped death. In some ways, recovering from compulsive gambling can feel like such an escape. In reality, there can be a close brush with physical death because a person's body is overwhelmed by the addiction, or because of an attempted suicide. In most cases there is the death of one's spirit. That was true for Virginia, who sought words to describe the meaning of her own recovery:

> *Recovery means, to me, changing from being dishonest, lying, stealing, being an unproductive human being to being honest and open-minded. And willing to open my heart and my mind to everything. Listening better . . . hearing, not only listening, but also hearing. And beginning to feel and care again instead of being*

numb. At several points along the way, I just absolutely had no feeling. I couldn't care less if the sun rose or shone. It's nice now to even hear a bird chirp—to recognize the bird singing. There's a woodpecker outside my door that I hear now. And he's probably been there for years and I never heard him. I mean, just the little things in life. ▪▪▪

Restoring a sense of joy in the little things in life is a common theme in the recovery process. It's sometimes described as what makes life worth living.

Managing the Bumps

Stopping compulsive gambling does solve a lot of really big problems. It's natural to expect that when these problems are gone or being taken care of, life will be beautiful again. However, most women experience some unexpected bumps in the road. Here's how one woman responded to the survey question asking if stopping gambling caused any negative effects:

▪▪▪ *They weren't negative, but they were unexpected. I always thought everything would be great if I could just stop gambling. The shakiest time in our marriage was when I stopped gambling and we addressed all the issues in our lives that needed addressing— WHEW!* ▪▪▪

Stopping gambling leaves a lot of time and emotional space for other life problems to become more visible. It's hard to deal with or even think about underlying issues while you are active in your addiction. When these issues start looming, an increase in irritability is likely to occur. You are no longer feeling guilty about neglecting your kids, but now that you are spending time with them, you find yourself cross and impatient. Women in the

Internet survey reported that in the initial period of recovery they experienced extreme boredom, nervousness, depression, feeling lazy and somewhat weak, anxiety, and doubts about being able to follow through with stopping gambling. These are all common early-recovery withdrawal symptoms that call for new coping skills.

Relearning old coping skills, and learning new ones, are often necessary for maintaining recovery. You can no longer deal with the stressors in your life by heading to the casino. Penny says, "You have to stop gambling first to get at your issues and have the strength to deal with them." She began to realize she was eating for comfort instead of nourishment, for example. This went on for two years in recovery, until she finally turned to Weight Watchers, followed its program, and reached her weight goal. Thus, she not only recognized a problem that she wasn't aware of before, but she also found a healthy way to work on it.

A person no doubt needs some comfort when stopping compulsive gambling. Many women who gave it up experienced a deep sense of loss, in spite of the devastation gambling had caused. "It was like losing your best friend or security blanket," said one woman in the Internet survey. Another complained of how difficult it was for her to "find any activity to fill the loneliness and boredom of my life like gambling did." Several women, like Penny, found themselves using food for comfort or increasing their use of alcohol and cigarettes. One wrote, "The underlying issues have not gone away, and sometimes I feel myself starting to substitute one addiction for another." Teresa initially felt like she was going crazy:

■■■ *At first all I could do was try to get through a day. I felt like I was going crazy. I was so restless. I guess it was an urge to gamble, although it was just an urge. I don't know how to describe it. It was just an urge of needing something. I just wanted to disappear and not hurt anymore. So that's the negatives, I guess, of getting into recovery. Climbing the walls of restlessness, anxiety, boredom, and anger . . . this lasted about six months.* ▪▪▪

The challenge of maintaining recovery under these conditions is an awesome one. On the one hand, you have to guard yourself from relapsing into gambling as an escape from bad feelings, and on the other hand, you have to gather your strength to reach out and learn new coping skills and new ways to reward yourself. Many women spoke of the need to do both, saying that stopping gambling by itself, although fundamental to the recovery process, was not enough. As Betty says, "There's a world of difference between abstinence and recovery." Part of that difference is what Twelve Step programs call the ability to "live life on life's terms." Here's how Marie described the meaning of her recovery:

▪▪▪ *At some point you lose the first flush of "Oh, wow, I got my life back, I'm getting things taken care of, I'm happy." Recovery doesn't mean you're always going to be happy. As far as what it does mean—it would just be being able to live a good life without having to gamble, without having to have a crutch to support you.* ▪▪▪

Mary's definition of recovery includes the willingness to change things about herself that she discovered were limitations:

▪▪▪ *Once I am abstinent and my head clears a little, then I am more aware of the problems I have to solve and the changes I have to make to my characteristics. I never knew until I stopped my addiction of compulsive gambling the things that I did wrong. Once I stopped it and listened to people, I became open-minded and I listened to what others were saying. I thought, "Gee, I did that too." And I thought, "These people changed, so maybe I can change, too." I guess that's when recovery started for me, and I learned how to be honest. I learned that honesty meant not just "cash register honesty" but being honest with myself, knowing what my limitations were.* ■■■

Guarding the Jewels: Avoiding Relapse

As Mary says, staying abstinent and avoiding relapse is what gives you the chance to do the other things that are needed to live a satisfying and meaningful life. Throughout the last four chapters, the women in the Internet study have shared the strategies that were successful for them in stopping gambling and avoiding relapse. Let's review a summary of their wisdom:

1. Don't underestimate the power of compulsive gambling.

The GA Combo Book describes gambling as "cunning, baffling, and powerful."[2] Sometimes it takes a few relapses to truly appreciate how difficult it can be to stop gambling compulsively. Irma, who is a Christian, described the powerful craving as "being under attack from Satan, and you're not thinking straight." You may not want to call it Satan, but it is a formidable force in your own mind. Sometimes your brain tells you that gambling is the only tried and true option for you to deal with emotional pain. Learning other options and coping strategies is essential to beating the powerful urge to escape through gambling.

It's also important to remind yourself often that compulsive gambling is a life-threatening problem. Not only do women lose their lives as they know them, their cars, houses, relationships, and jobs, but they can completely lose hope, contemplate suicide, and even carry it out. One of the benefits of quitting, said one woman, was that she "no longer considered suicide as the only alternative to gambling." Others die from heart attacks, high blood pressure, strokes, and other illnesses brought on by extreme stress. Underestimating the destructive power of compulsive gambling ("Oh, it wasn't all that bad") is a tip-off that you may be on the road to relapse.

Twelve Step programs have a saying: "You can get off the elevator at any time," meaning you don't have to go all the way to the bottom before you quit. For whatever reason, when you are gambling compulsively, you are on the "down" elevator. At the bottom is "prison, insanity, or death," according to GA. If you keep on gambling or go back to it, it's important to realize that's where you are headed.

2. Pile it on.

Because the urge to go back to gambling "just one more time" can be so very strong, it's helpful to pile on lots of maintenance strategies. Putting yourself in a position to be exposed, every day, to some kind of recovery focus helps retrain your mind to embrace abstinence, not gambling. This can be in the form of an inspirational reading or meditation to start and end the day; attendance at GA meetings; participation in professional treatment programs; getting together by phone, text, or in person with someone else in recovery; practicing cognitive techniques; or deliberately finding time to commune with the spiritual side of life. This is the *work* part of the recovery process, and is especially important in the first few months. Susan finds there is no easy way:

> ▪▪▪ *Everyone wants a pill, they want a shot, they don't want to do the work. A person just has to . . . I tell people to try to look for a positive every day that they can keep in front of them. Even if it's just that they don't have to lie to somebody for one day. Whatever they consider the smallest success, it's piling up those successes*

every day. It's like the angel and the devil sitting on your shoulder.
The more things you can pile up on the angel side, the less you're
going to want to listen to the other side. ▪▪▪

3. Practice cognitive techniques.

Chapter 7 described a number of cognitive strategies that have
been found helpful in stopping relapses before they start. One of the
most powerful is thinking through the consequences of relapse.

Many compulsive gamblers are not used to pausing and thinking at all when they get the urge. Betty "never really thought about
it all, I just went gambling." Instead, practice visualizing what it's
going to be like in reality. Betty now thinks about how "if I go
gamble, I am going to walk out of the casino and feel like crap
and it's going to get me down and I am going to have to start all
over again." Other cognitive techniques include writing out the
short- and long-term consequences of continuing to gamble, using
the ABC approach to writing out what triggers you to think about
gambling, your irrational thoughts and behaviors that encourage
you to gamble, and countering them with the consequences of what
really happens.

Another cognitive strategy that is also advocated in GA and
treatment programs is to structure your time with a daily plan of
what you will do to support your recovery every day. "Exposure,
exposure, exposure" is the mantra of the recovery landscape. Tara
read the GA Combo Book every day, as well as a daily meditation
from a small book called *A Day at a Time*.[3] She says:

▪▪▪ *I actually established a ritual that every morning the first thing*
I would do is say the Serenity Prayer, read from A Day at a Time,
and try to focus on positive things. During the day, I would go to
websites on the Internet that have inspirational sayings and stories,
and I would post and write. I began to re-find the kind of music

I used to listen to. I listened to classical music or contemporary Christian music; something that would keep me focused on positive recovery things. Whatever it took to calm my mind, that's what I did. ▪▪▪

All of the cognitive strategies are designed to help you strengthen your mind to be able to withstand the siren call of gambling. In order to help her stay aware of the false thoughts from the siren, Judy, a single woman in a professional job, made a list of typical phrases that start going through her mind when she is rationalizing a relapse. These include:

1. "This will be the last time."
2. "I should win this time; I've been losing for so long."
3. "Just a few hundred and then I'll leave."
4. "Nobody will know."
5. "It's my money, I can do with it what I want."
6. "It's my life, I can fuck it up if I want to."
7. "I'll quit after this."
8. "I deserve a break (celebration) for a few hours . . . I've earned it."
9. "At least I won't be home all by myself."
10. "Nobody cares what happens to me anyway."
11. "I'll be caught up with payday loans within three weeks, so no problem."
12. "I don't have anything to do with this money except pay back credit cards and I'll do that over time."
13. "All I need to win is a couple hundred, then I can pay the cable bill."
14. "The casino owes me, after all the money I've put in."
15. "Everybody else has a life, all I have is work, work, work."
16. "[*Fill in the name*] just pisses me off! What right does he/she

have to act that way!! I'll just give myself a little break and forget the whole thing."

17. "I can't pay that bill anyway, might as well risk it."
18. "What have I got to lose except my misery?"

You might want to make your own list of dangerous thinking habits that could convince you to gamble again (in recovery circles, this is often referred to as "stinking thinking"). Your list will look a little different from Judy's. Start by writing down the ideas that sneak up on you to soften you up for a gambling episode; doing so will help the recovering part of your brain become alert to these danger signals. Judy put her list up on her refrigerator so she could remind herself of the power of the addicted part of her brain when it starts craving to gamble.

4. Put barriers between you and gambling.

Physical barriers are not foolproof. A problem gambler has already learned to find ways around many barriers in order to feed the compulsion. In reality, banning yourself from the casino, turning your finances over to others, and distancing yourself from people who gamble are only effective barriers if you choose to make them so. However, when *you* are the one choosing to put these barriers up in the first place, you don't have to rebel and try to circumvent them.

Donna, who knew her own wiliness, put double barriers in place. She not only handed over her checks to someone else, she wrote the check cashing companies at the casinos and requested they not approve any more of her checks. She also asked them never to change her nonapproval status, even if she made the request. They honored her wishes. Donna knows this because once in the middle of a relapse, she tried to convince them to approve a check. They didn't, and the refusal stopped her relapse. She was able to go home and regroup.

Another way of developing barriers is by using the time–opportunity–money (TOM) equation. Laura explained that if you have all three of those in place, you are likely to gamble. But if you can remove one of them, you won't. The easiest thing to remove is money, by putting someone else in charge of your finances. Time can be removed through work, daily schedules, and activities with others. Opportunity can be removed through banning oneself from casinos and removing check privileges and closing or removing your name from checking accounts, for example. Of course, it's never quite that simple, but looking at your daily TOM gives you a way to regularly evaluate your current state of vulnerability and make adjustments.

Stopping a Relapse and Coming Back to Recovery

Let's say that in spite of your best efforts, you find yourself gambling again and bitterly regretting it. Feelings of helplessness, shame, and remorse dominate your thoughts. You want to hide from everyone, especially those people who supported you during your darkest hours of early recovery. What can you do now? Because relapse can be such an emotionally devastating experience, it's best to have a good, solid plan in place for how to stop it or cut it short.

Don't panic. To begin building back your confidence and self-esteem, keep in mind that relapse is considered a normal part of the recovery process (see chapter 5). Although it may feel like the end of the world, it isn't. The only way it becomes the end of the world is if you keep right on gambling and give up on recovery. Just like a toddler has to fall down many times before successfully walking and running, a person hooked on gambling has to go through a process to get thoroughly unhooked.

Emergency measures may have to be taken to stop the episode. Otherwise, the relapse will stop when you run out of money. If you are in the casino or card room, it may help to force yourself to go somewhere quieter (a restroom, your car) for a moment to review what's happening. Ask yourself how you are feeling about losing. How are you really feeling about being back at the casino or card room? Breaking the spin for five minutes can help you find the determination to walk out. Call someone who will understand. Even if you can't walk out or call, eventually you will run out of money, which temporarily stops the relapse.

In a Canadian study, researchers Kylie Thygesen and David Hodgins interviewed sixty compulsive gamblers in Calgary, Alberta, about their strategies and reasons for stopping a relapse episode.[4] The most frequently stated reason was lack of money—either running out of money or lacking funds in general. After that, participants cited negative feelings: disliking the feeling of losing (no high) and feeling guilt, shame, and self-hatred when they thought about their relapse. Next came thinking about the true nature of gambling odds, and examining the effect of gambling on relationships. The authors agree that relapse is a complex process that we don't have all the answers to, and that more study in this area is needed.

However that relapse episode stops, when it does stop, the important thing is to put the focus back on recovery. Robert Ladouceur and his colleagues, who work with compulsive gamblers in Quebec, recommend the following:[5]

1. Frame the relapse as an event that can be avoided in the future. In other words, it is not a pattern that once started will not stop, and it doesn't indicate you are a total failure as a human being. It is a mistake you can learn from.

2. Remember the progress you have made and the number of times you've wanted to gamble and yet have not. How did you do that? What were the strategies that worked for you?

3. Analyze what happened. What was going on, or not going on, that contributed to your vulnerability? What do you need to add or subtract to be more successful? Imagine the scenario with a different ending—one where you did not gamble. What helped you resist the urge?

4. Ask for help. Your support network can help you through encouragement and understanding. They can help you put this in perspective and get back to work. Even if you feel ashamed and unworthy, reach out to those who know what the struggle is all about.

Developing New Coping Skills: "The Courage to Change the Things I Can . . ."

The above words from the Serenity Prayer relate to the third part of the recovery recipe: gathering your strength to reach out and learn new coping skills and new ways to reward yourself. Quitting gambling leaves a tremendous void. Not only are you weighed down with time you didn't have before; you begin to notice that your coping skills are rusty after months and years of neglect. In addition, things that used to interest you seem diluted and bland; they don't compare to the intense fix provided by gambling.

At some point after quitting, most women in the Internet study found it necessary to evaluate the quality of their lives and to plan ways to make it better. Many did this through the Twelve Steps of GA. Some evaluated using professional help, others began to view their lives through religious values, and still others took stock on their own. Art Jacobs, a professional addiction counselor in Spokane, Washington, uses a values clarification exercise to help gamblers focus on what is truly important them.[6] He emphasizes that finding interests and passions other than gambling is critical to maintaining abstinence. Whatever that is, its strength needs to be equal to or greater than the addiction to gambling. Jacobs asks his clients to look at their major life areas (such as finances; mental, physical, and emotional health; relationships; spirituality; recreational pursuits; career; and preparing for retirement) and assign meaning to each area. Asking yourself a number of questions helps you with this exercise:

- Is there any area you could live without?
- How does gambling affect each area?
- Is what you are doing right now enhancing or detracting from your quality of life?
- How would you like to be functioning in each area?
- What are the roadblocks to improving functioning?
- What are the goals and objectives that will help you achieve your ideal self?

According to Jacobs, this is one of the most meaningful exercises for people recovering from addictions, because it helps them change their reward system to practices that are healthy. Instead of acting on the old idea that going to the casino will improve your finances, for example, you may have in place a competing, more important goal of paying back a relative. Each time you make a payment, you are giving yourself a small reward. At the same time you have strengthened the values that will help you stay out of the old addictive thinking patterns.

In chapter 7, we saw how some women were learning new coping skills and moving toward their ideal self through professional counseling. For Joan, this was particularly important. She says, "Deciding to get into a counseling group was the most important support two years into my recovery. I felt I would have stayed 'stuck' and continued in old patterns and possibly returned to gambling if I hadn't felt complete trust in my counselor and the confidentiality in my women's therapy group." For many of the women in the Internet study, Gamblers Anonymous was an important support for learning and relearning coping skills. As one woman reported, GA "helped with breaking the wall down, and removing numbness of thinking." Another commented that GA "helped me develop coping skills and how to handle feelings in a healthy way, instead of escaping."

Another avenue for learning new coping skills and finding new rewards for yourself is to reach out to friends, old and new. Many women don't even realize how lonely they were while gambling compulsively, until they stop gambling and start connecting with others. It's a common worry—that loneliness and boredom will follow when one quits gambling—but it's unfounded, as long as one makes even a slight effort to counter it. One person in the survey even met her "clean and sober husband" in recovery, and staying abstinent is part of their daily life.

New friends who understand and don't judge you are immediately available through Gamblers Anonymous or professional treatment programs. Some women found friends by reconnecting with a worship congregation, or by finding a new one that would forgive and understand the mistakes they had made. Others found friends through Internet sites and message boards for compulsive gamblers. Old friends who you had avoided during the compulsive gambling days are happy to see you again, unless you've borrowed money from them and haven't paid them back. Even if that is the case, you can start the process of a payment plan that will eventually help to rebuild trust in your relationship.

The honorable practice of being of service to others usually goes out the window with compulsive gambling. You are too wrapped up in your own addiction to spend much time thinking of others. However, as part of the maintenance plan, many women found that giving time and service to others was a satisfying reward in recovery. Glenda found that going public with her story was an important part of building her self-esteem:

> ■■■ *I do some public speaking about my story and the help and hope that GA offers those who still suffer. This has been appreciated in our community, and my husband is proud of my ability to attack the problems at hand and make our family name more respected in the community. He is proud of my ability to now admit the disease, although he doesn't completely understand it. But that's ok. For once in my life, this issue is about me and me alone.* ■■■

Other women expressed that as a result of their recovery, they were able to "help others and show them how to stop gambling," "be a contributing member of my community," and "support others, young and old, who are addicted to gambling." Several women told of their intention to go back to school for training in addiction counseling.

Reclaiming old interests is another method of finding new rewards. Although former pursuits may not initially appear to compare to the glitz and drama of gambling, many women found that picking up former hobbies was a concrete support to maintaining their recovery. Joanne found she had to look for "something to spend her time on." She began to "redevelop some hobbies that I had abandoned. My sister and I used to do craft-like hobbies together, and I've always liked sewing, so I started to reclaim some of these things." Others report it is indeed possible to enjoy the things you used to enjoy, such as reading, watching movies, and doing activities with your kids, family, or friends. One woman noted "spending time at home playing with my cat doing 'normal-people' things like cooking, cleaning, reading, and email."

It is not easy to do both things at once: guard yourself from relapse into gambling, and gather your strength to reach out and learn new coping skills and new ways to reward yourself. In the face of this challenge, many of the women found spiritual support to be critical for maintaining recovery.

Spirituality and Maintenance

What does it mean to practice spirituality? The women in the Internet study answered in diverse and interesting ways. For Marilyn, spirituality is all about connection. She says, "Today my definition of spirituality is how I connect with my Higher Power, with other members of the program, with my family, with my employer. It's my connection. I can have a spiritual feeling when I am driving down the highway if I see a bumper sticker on a car that says 'First Things First' or 'Easy Does It'. And that's a little spiritual connection for me. Sometimes I'm uptight, I walk into a GA meeting and I look around at my friends, and there is that connection. Isn't that beautiful?"

For women who are GA members, spirituality is a fundamental part of practicing the Twelve Step program, regardless of what form it takes. Let's look at the language of the Steps (which are incidentally written in past tense, as a collective expression of effective practices). In GA, Step One is "We admitted we were powerless over gambling—that our lives had become unmanageable"; Step Two is "came to believe that a Power greater than ourselves could restore us to a normal way of thinking and living"; and Step Three is "made a decision to turn our will and our lives over to the care of this Power of our own understanding." In Step Eleven, we "sought through prayer and meditation to improve our conscious contact with God as we understood Him, praying only for knowledge of His will for us and the power to carry that out."[7]

It's clear that a spiritual stance on life is to be practiced as part of the GA program; however, women who were not involved in

GA also expressed that some kind of spiritual connection was helpful. There is a lot of flexibility in what that means and how spirituality is understood. Marie says she could practice Step Two by believing that the Power greater than ourselves "doesn't have to be God." For her, the Power was the "tremendous Power in the GA group," and her sponsor. Before she could even come to that understanding, she says she had to "throw away" her conception of God as a youth. "I come from a kind of hostile, Baptist, teenage group, and that is not the God I believe in now. All I had to know was that there was somebody in the shadow back there."

Some found recovery support in some kind of organized religion. One person found a "recovery church" that especially recruited members of the recovering community, regardless of what kind of addiction. Another woman says she was grateful to her gambling addiction because it led her back to finding God and religion. She says, "GA led me directly to God. Now I am a born-again Christian, so in a way, I am grateful for my addiction. Prior to my addiction, I didn't believe in God." Kelly thought that GA's principles were very much like the values of Christianity, such as forgiveness and making amends. She sees gambling as "a temptation, a battle, and a sin." She "depends on God and Jesus to give me the strength and the help."

Other women had problems with organized religion. Jane goes to church but has a feeling that the other members are disapproving. She says, "I'm having a hard time going out in front of people, because I feel like they are looking at me saying 'Oh, look, there she is, she gambled everything away.' Everybody knows about the gambling thing and I feel they look down on me for it." Sarah went back to church in her small community but didn't tell anyone about her gambling problem or recovery. "It's not that I'm ashamed I was a gambler," she says, "it's just that a lot of people just don't understand." Still others did not have a belief in a power outside of themselves, but instead focused on nurturing "inner strengths."

When asked what has been the most satisfying part of the recovery process, many women thought they most valued regaining a sense of spirituality, or gaining one for the first time. For example:

- "Serenity, do not judge, belief in a Higher Power."
- "Learning more about God and how he has worked miracles in my life without my even realizing it."
- "Learning to love myself, my life, to appreciate the smallest, most wonderful gifts that God has given to each of us every day."
- "That I have faith again in God and the good in the world."

Clearly, some sense of spirituality was helpful in recovery, regardless of how this was practiced. As Betty says, "I call my Higher Power 'God,' whether that be a He, She, or It, it doesn't matter. I look at my relationship with my Higher Power as a partnership with God. And God is the senior partner."

The Meaning of Recovery

Throughout this chapter, various women have expressed their own meanings of recovery. Those beliefs and interpretations are as different as the women themselves. A favorite of mine sums it all up in one sentence: "Knowing myself and not thinking I was from another planet." Coming back to this world, with all its complexities, shadings, and challenges, is a tremendous achievement for a compulsive gambler.

To illustrate what coming back to this world looks like, addiction counselor Art Jacobs draws a great big circle. "This is your world before gambling," he says, "and within the circle are all your relationships, interests, responsibilities, values, finances, problems, and successes." Then he draws a tiny black dot. "This is your world while you are gambling compulsively," he says. "This is how small and narrow it gets. Going to the casino, coming back from the casino, trying to cover your losses, finding money, losing money." It's likely the only two feelings you have are anxiety and despair.

Making that tiny black dot become a whole, imperfect, glorious world again was indeed worth the work and struggle for the women you've met through this book. That is the hope they pass on to you through their stories. Each of them had to learn how to cope in a new world without the instant escape of gambling when things got a bit rough. Each had to learn ways of facing "life on life's terms." For most of these women, life's terms were very difficult in early recovery. Many faced financial ruin, broken relationships, and emotional rawness after years of being numb. But they did it. Many found hope through people they didn't even know prior to stopping. These women are not "Superwomen." They are ordinary women taken to the depths of despair and hopelessness. Then they took a small step in the direction of recovery, and then another step, and another, until they finally put together some time and freedom. If you can take even one little part of their experience and add it to the side of you that wants to take your life back from gambling—and keep it—your own hope will begin to grow. You can start with one small step, just as they did.

Notes

■ ■ ■

Chapter 1

1. Pew Research Center, *Gambling: As the Take Rises, So Does Public Concern* (Washington, DC: Pew Research Center, 2006), http://pewresearch.org/assets/social/pdf/Gambling.pdf (retrieved Feb. 7, 2009).

2. K. Peterson, *48 States Raking In Gambling Proceeds* (Washington, DC: Pew Research Center, May 23, 2006), www.stateline.org (retrieved Aug. 20, 2008).

3. National Gambling Impact Study Commission, *Final Report* (Washington, DC: U.S. Government Printing Office, 1999), www.ncfamily.org/specialngisc.html (retrieved Feb. 15, 2009).

4. Pew Research Center, *Gambling.*

5. Earl L. Grinols, *Gambling in America: Costs and Benefits* (Cambridge, England: Cambridge University Press, 2004).

6. Committee on the Social and Economic Impact of Pathological Gambling and Committee on Law and Justice, *Pathological Gambling: A Critical Review* (Washington, DC: National Academy Press, 1999). This report is also available online at www.nap.edu.

7. Rachel A. Volberg, "Has There Been a 'Feminization' of Gambling and Problem Gambling in the United States?" *eGambling* 8 (May 2003), www.camh.net/egambling/issue8/feature/index.html (retrieved Feb. 7, 2009).

8. Arizona Council on Compulsive Gambling, "Gambling Got You Down?" (2007), www.azccg.org/home.htm (retrieved Feb. 7, 2009).

9. Connecticut Council on Problem Gambling, *Reports from Helpline* (2007), www.ccpg.org/reports.html (retrieved Aug. 21. 2008).

10. Anonymous, "Reflections on Problem Gambling Therapy with Female Clients," *eGambling* 8 (May 2003), www.camh.net/egambling/issue8/first_person/index.html (retrieved Feb. 7, 2009).

11. Roberta Boughton, "A Feminist Slant on Counseling the Female Gambler: Key Issues and Tasks," *eGambling* 8 (May 2003), www.camh.net/egambling/issue8/clinic/boughton/index.html (retrieved Jan. 21, 2008).

Chapter 2

1. K. Trevorrow and S. Moore, "The Association between Loneliness, Social Isolation and Women's Electronic Gaming Machine Gambling," *Journal of Gambling Studies* 14, no. 3 (1998), 263–84.

2. Arizona Council on Compulsive Gambling, *Action or Escape Gamblers,* www.azccg.org/a_types/types.htm (retrieved Dec. 15, 2008).

3. Christopher Donahue and Jon Grant, "Stress and Impulsive Behaviors," in *Stress and Addiction: Biological and Psychological Mechanisms,* ed. Mustafa al'Absi, 191–206 (New York: Academic Press, 2007).

4. N. Petry and K. Steinberg, "Childhood Maltreatment in Male and Female Treatment-Seeking Pathological Gamblers," *Psychology of Addictive Behaviors* 19, no. 2 (2005), 226–29.

5. R. Netemeyer, S. Burton, L. Cole, D. Williamson, N. Zucker, L. Bertman, and G. Diefenbach, "Characteristics and Beliefs Associated with Probable Pathological Gambling: A Pilot Study with Implications for the National Gambling Impact and Policy Commission," *Journal of Public Policy & Marketing* 17, no. 2 (1998), 147–60.

6. Diane R. Davis and Lisa Avery, "Women Who Have Taken Their Lives Back from Compulsive Gambling: Results from an Online Survey," *Journal of Social Work Practice in the Addictions* 4, no. 1 (2004), 61–80.

7. National Council on Problem Gambling, "The Neurobiology of Pathological Gambling: Proceedings of the 19th Annual Conference on Prevention, Research, and Treatment of Problem Gambling," New Orleans, June 23–25, 2005, *Journal of Gambling Issues* 15.

8. C. D. Fiorillo, "The Uncertain Nature of Dopamine," *Molecular Psychiatry* 9, no. 2 (2004), 122–23.

9. National Council on Problem Gambling, "The Neurobiology of Pathological Gambling."

10. *ScienceDaily*/Duke University, "How Brain Gives Special Resonance to Emotional Memories," *ScienceDaily* June 10, 2004, www.science daily.com/releases/2004/06/040610081107.htm (retrieved Jan. 3, 2008).

11. National Gambling Impact Study Commission, *Final Report* (Washington, DC: U.S. Government Printing Office, 1999), www.ncfamily .org/specialngisc.html (retrieved Feb. 15, 2009).

12. M. Walker, *The Psychology of Gambling* (New York: Pergamon Press, 1992).

13. E. Hollander, A. Buchalter, and C. DeCaria, "Pathological Gambling," *The Psychiatric Clinics of North America* 23, no. 3 (2000), 623–28.

14. National Gambling Impact Study Commission, *Final Report*.

15. Gamblers Anonymous, *Gamblers Anonymous* (Los Angeles: Gamblers Anonymous, 2007).

Chapter 3

1. Committee on the Social and Economic Impact of Pathological Gambling and Committee on Law and Justice, *Pathological Gambling.*

2. Ibid., 2.

3. American Psychiatric Association (APA), *Diagnostic and Statistical Manual of Mental Disorders, Text Revision*, 4th ed. (Washington, DC: APA, 2000).

4. Gamblers Anonymous, *Gamblers Anonymous: A New Beginning*, 4th ed. (Los Angeles: Gamblers Anonymous, 2000), 1.

5. The Gamblers Anonymous Twenty Questions are available online at www.gamblersanonymous.org.

6. Sarah Brown and Louise Coventry, *Queen of Hearts* (Victoria, Australia: Financial and Consumer Rights Council, 1997).

7. APA, *Diagnostic and Statistical Manual of Mental Disorders, Text Revision* (4th ed.), 674.

8. H. Lesieur and S. Blume, "The South Oaks Gambling Screen: A New Instrument for the Identification of Pathological Gamblers," *Journal of Gambling Studies* 12 (1987), 129–42.

9. H. Lesieur and S. Blume, "South Oaks Gambling Screen," www
.in.gov/judiciary/ijlap/docs/south-oaks-gambling-screen.pdf (retrieved
Sept. 10, 2008).

10. Gam-Anon Family Groups, "Are You Living with a Compulsive
Gambler?" www.gam-anon.org/living.htm (retrieved Sept. 15, 2008).

Chapter 4

1. H. Tavares, M. Zilberman, F. Beites, and V. Gentil, "Gender
Differences in Gambling Progression," *Journal of Gambling Studies*
17 (2001), 151–59. See also M. Potenza, M. Steinberg, S. McLaughlin,
R. Wu, B. Rounsaville, and S. O'Malley, "Gender-Related Differences in
the Characteristics of Problem Gamblers Using a Gambling Helpline,"
American Journal of Psychiatry 158 (2001), 1500–05.

2. Lisa Avery and Diane R. Davis, "Women's Recovery from Compulsive Gambling: Formal and Informal Supports," *Journal of Social
Work Practice in the Addictions* 8, no. 2 (2008).

3. Ibid.

4. M. Battersby, B. Tolchard, M. Scurrah, and L. Thomas, "Suicide
Ideation and Behavior in People with Pathological Gambling Attending
a Treatment Program," *International Journal of Mental Health and
Addiction* 4, no. 3 (2006), 233–46. See also D. Hodgins and K. Thygesen,
"Quitting Again: Motivations and Strategies for Terminating Gambling
Relapses," *eGambling* 9, (2003).

5. Gamblers Anonymous, *Gamblers Anonymous: A New Beginning.*

Chapter 5

1. James Prochaska and Carlo DiClemente, "The Transtheoretical
Approach," in *Handbook of Eclectic Psychotherapy*, 3rd ed., ed. J. C.
Norcross, 163–200 (New York: Brunner/Mazel, 1986).

2. M. Griffiths, "Betting Your Life on It," *British Medical Journal*
329, no. 6 (2004), 1055–56.

3. Boughton, "A Feminist Slant on Counseling the Female Gambler."

4. R. Longley, "Education Greatly Boosts Women's Earnings: Report," About.com: US Government Info (May 2005), http://usgovinfo .about.com/od/censusandstatistics/a/womenpayed.htm (retrieved Jan. 21, 2008).

5. Boughton, "A Feminist Slant on Counseling the Female Gambler."

6. Anonymous, "Reflections on Problem Gambling Therapy with Female Clients."

7. Avery and Davis, "Women's Recovery from Compulsive Gambling."

8. D. Hodgins and N. el-Guebaly, "Retrospective and Prospective Reports of Precipitants to Relapse in Pathological Gambling," *Journal of Consulting and Clinical Psychology* 72, no. 1 (2004), 72–80.

9. Avery and Davis, "Women's Recovery from Compulsive Gambling."

10. Sarah Brown and Louise Coventry, *Queen of Hearts.*

Chapter 6

1. Arizona Council on Compulsive Gambling, www.azccg.org (retrieved June 16, 2000).

2. Robert Custer, "Gambling and Addiction," in *Drug Dependent Patients: Treatment and Research,* ed. Robert. Craig and L. L. Baker, 367–81 (Springfield, IL: Charles C. Thomas, 1982).

3. Avery and Davis, "Women's Recovery from Compulsive Gambling."

4. Gamblers Anonymous, *Gamblers Anonymous,* 2.

5. Ibid., 6.

6. Ibid., 2.

7. Ibid., 17.

8. Gamblers Anonymous, *Towards 90 Days* (Los Angeles: Gamblers Anonymous, 1999), 3.

9. Peter Ferentzy and Wayne Skinner, "Gamblers Anonymous: A Critical Review of the Literature," *eGambling* 9, no. 1 (2003), www

.camh.net/egambling/issue9v1/research/ferentszy/index.html (retrieved Feb. 28, 2008).

10. R. M. Stewart and R. I. F. Brown, "An Outcome Study of Gamblers Anonymous," *British Journal of Psychiatry* 152 (1988), 284–88.

11. Avery and Davis, "Women's Recovery from Compulsive Gambling."

12. Ibid.

13. Ibid.

14. Ibid.

15. Gamblers Anonymous, *Working the Steps* (Los Angeles: Gamblers Anonymous, 2007).

16. Gamblers Anonymous, *Gamblers Anonymous*, 3.

17. Katherine van Wormer and Diane Rae Davis, *Addiction Treatment: A Strengths Perspective*, 2nd ed. (Belmont, CA: Thomson Brooks/Cole, 2008).

18. Gamblers Anonymous, *Working the Steps*, 1.

19. Patrick Carnes, *A Gentle Path Through the Twelve Steps: The Classic Guide for All People in the Process of Recovery* (Center City, MN: Hazelden, 1993).

20. Gamblers Anonymous, *Working the Steps*, 3.

21. Ibid., 5.

22. Ibid., 7.

23. Ibid., 9.

24. Kevin Griffin, *One Breath at a Time: Buddhism and the Twelve Steps* (New York: Rodale, 2004).

25. Stephanie Covington, *A Woman's Way through the Twelve Steps* (Center City, MN: Hazelden, 1994), 79.

26. Gamblers Anonymous, *Working the Steps*, 13.

27. Ibid., 15.

28. Ibid., 17.

29. Ibid., 23.

30. Gamblers Anonymous, *Sharing Recovery Through Gamblers Anonymous* (Los Angeles: Gamblers Anonymous, 1999).

Chapter 7

1. RealMentalHealth.com, *Women and Gambling Addiction*, www.realmentalhealth.com/addictions/gambling_women.asp (retrieved Dec. 15, 2008).

2. Mark Moran, "Gambling with Addiction" WebMD Medical News, www.webMD.com/news/20010516/gambling-with-addiction (retrieved March 5, 2008).

3. Avery and Davis, "Women's Recovery from Compulsive Gambling."

4. Robert Ladouceur, Caroline Sylvain, Claude Boutin, and Celine Doucet, *Understanding and Treating the Pathological Gambler* (West Sussex, England: John Wiley & Sons, 2002).

5. Van Wormer and Davis, *Addiction Treatment,* 2nd ed.

6. Ladouceur et al., *Understanding and Treating the Pathological Gambler.*

7. Committee on the Social and Economic Impact of Pathological Gambling and Committee on Law and Justice, *Pathological Gambling.*

8. N. Dowling, D. Smith, and T. Thomas, "Treatment of Female Pathological Gambling: The Efficacy of a Cognitive-Behavioral Approach," *Gambling Studies* 22, no. 4 (2006), 355–72.

9. Committee on the Social and Economic Impact of Pathological Gambling and Committee on Law and Justice, *Pathological Gambling.*

10. W. Rhodes, J. Norman, S. Langenbahn, P. Harmon, and D. Deal, *Evaluation of the Minnesota State-Funded Compulsive Gambling Treatment Programs, Final Report, July 21, 1997* (Cambridge, MA: Abt Associates, Inc., 1997).

11. Richard Rosenthal, "The Role of Medication in the Treatment of Pathological Gambling: Bridging the Gap between Research and Practice," *eGambling* 10 (2004), www.camh.net/egambling/issue10/ejgi_10_rosenthal.html (retrieved Feb. 7, 2008).

12. Natasha Schull, "Machines, Medication, Modulation: Circuits of Dependency and Self-Care in Las Vegas," *Culture, Medicine and Psychiatry* 30 (2006), 223–47; quoted passage, 234.

13. Rosenthal, "The Role of Medication."

14. Avery and Davis, "Women's Recovery from Compulsive Gambling."

15. Anonymous, "Reflections on Problem Gambling Therapy with Female Clinets."

Chapter 8

1. W. Slutske, "Natural Recovery and Treatment-Seeking in Pathological Gambling: Results of Two U.S. National Surveys," *American Journal of Psychiatry* 163 (2), 297–302.

2. W. Cloud and R. Granfield, "Natural Recovery from Substance Dependency: Lessons for Treatment Providers," *Journal of Social Work Practice in the Addictions* 1, no. 1 (2001), 83–104.

3. Roberta Boughton and K. Brewster, "Voices of Women Who Gamble in Ontario: A Survey of Women's Gambling, Barriers to Treatment and Service Needs." Ministry of Health and Long-Term Care Problem Gambling Unit, Addiction Programs, Ontario, Canada. The report is available online at www.gamblingresearch.org.

4. Avery and Davis, "Women's Recovery from Compulsive Gambling."

5. D. Hodgins, S. Currie, and N. el-Guebaly, "Motivational Enhancement and Self-Help Treatments for Problem Gambling," *Journal of Consulting Clinical Psychology* 69, (2001), 50–7.

Chapter 9

1. N. Dowling , D. Smith, and T. Thomas, "The Family Functioning of Female Pathological Gamblers," *Journal of Family Psychology* 8 (2007), 432–46.

2. Avery and Davis, "Women's Recovery from Compulsive Gambling."

3. Gam-Anon, "Our Purpose," www.gam-anon.org/purpose.htm (retrieved June 13, 2007).

Chapter 10

1. Avery and Davis, "Women's Recovery from Compulsive Gambling."

2. Gamblers Anonymous, *Combo Book* (Los Angeles: Gamblers Anonymous, 2000).

3. Gamblers Anonymous, *A Day at a Time* (Center City, MN: Hazelden, 1976).

4. Kylie Thygesen and David Hodgins, "Quitting Again: Motivations and Strategies for Terminating Gambling Relapses," *eGambling* 9 (October 2003), www.camh.net/egambling/issue9/research/thygesen (retrieved June 15, 2008).

5. Ladouceur et al., *Understanding and Treating the Pathological Gambler.*

6. Personal communication, June 19, 2008.

7. Gamblers Anonymous, *Working the Steps.*

Resources

■ ■ ■

National Council on Problem Gambling
www.ncpgambling.org
The purpose of the National Council is to increase public awareness of pathological gambling, ensure the widespread availability of treatment for problem gamblers and their families, and encourage research and programs for prevention and education. This Web site is full of important and authoritative information on the nature of problem gambling, certified counselors in each state, State Councils and how to reach them, literature on gambling problems and their solutions, and much more.

Arizona Council on Compulsive Gambling
www.azccg.org
Although there are many excellent state problem gambling Web sites, the Arizona one offers an entire version in Spanish. The site also features information on special groups of gamblers: females, males, teens, seniors, and more.

Women Helping Women
www.femalegamblers.info
Offering all kinds of help and support to women with gambling problems, this Web site was developed by Marilyn L. and Betty C., two recovering gamblers from Arizona. Each month a newsletter is published containing several stories written by women in recovery on such topics as dealing with boredom, families, how they recovered, and so on. Many newsletters also have related articles by professionals in the field. The Web site has a newsletter archive and provides links to other resources on the Web, recommended books, and articles on gambling.

Alberta Gaming Research Institute
http://gaming.uleth.ca

Harvard Institute for Research on Pathological Gambling
and Related Disorders
www.divisiononaddictions.org

Both of these Web sites offer government and research publications that are academic in nature. They provide a good look at
the types of current research that are now being conducted in the
United States and Canada.

Appendix

■ ■ ■

Demographic, Gambling Behavior, and Recovery Survey
"Women who took their lives back from compulsive gambling" Project

Diane Rae Davis, Ph.D.
Principal Investigator, Professor, Social Work
Eastern Washington University

This survey was posted on the Internet in 2000–2001, and this book is based in part on the stories of the women who responded. For the reader's reference, it is reprinted here with only very minor alterations.

DEMOGRAPHICS

Age
     1. Under 18
     2. 18–20
     3. 20–25
     4. 25–30
     5. 30–35
     6. 35–40
     7. 40–45
     8. 45–50
     9. 50–55
     10. 55–60
     11. 60–65
     12. 65–70
     13. 70–75

With which of the following groups or group do you most identify? Check all that apply.

1. White
2. African American
3. Hispanic/Latino
4. Asian American
5. Native American
6. Pacific Islander
7. Prefer not to answer
8. Other _____

Current Marital Status

1. Never Married
2. Married
3. Divorced/Separated
4. Widowed
5. Cohabitating

Which of the following represents the highest level of education that you have completed?

1. Some high school or less
2. High school graduate
3. Some college
4. Bachelor's degree
5. Some graduate study
6. Graduate degree
7. Doctorate degree

Current Employment Status

1. Professional
2. Manager-Proprietor
3. Clerical-Sales

4. Skilled Blue Collar

5. Semi-Skilled Operator

6. Food Service Worker

7. Laborer

8. Farm Worker

9. Unemployed

10. Student

11. Disabled

12. Housewife

13. Retired

Specific current occupation _____

Income Data

Annual income before taxes (excluding partner or husband)

$ _____

Annual family income before taxes (including partner or husband) $ _____

Are you currently buying a home or a homeowner?

Yes   No

Children/Stepchildren

Do you have children or stepchildren living at home at least part of the time?

Yes   No

Please tell me what state you currently reside in:

_____

Family History

Which of the following describes your experience of your family as a child growing up?

1. Healthy, loving family

  2. Some problems, but mostly problem-free

  3. Problems of medium difficulty

  4. Family problems that were overwhelming at times

  5. Problems so severe that the family couldn't cope most of
the time

Which of the following people in your family has (or had) a gambling problem? Check all that apply.

  1. Spouse or partner

  2. Mother

  3. Father

  4. Maternal grandmother

  5. Maternal grandfather

  6. Paternal grandmother

  7. Paternal grandfather

  8. Sister

  9. Brother

 10. Child or children

 11. Aunt or uncle

 12. No one in my family has had a gambling problem

Which of the following people in your family have a history of alcoholism or drug addiction? Check all that apply.

  1. Spouse or partner

  2. Mother

  3. Father

  4. Maternal grandmother

  5. Maternal grandfather

  6. Paternal grandmother

  7. Paternal grandfather

  8. Sister

  9. Brother

10. Child or children

11. Aunt or uncle

12. No one in my family has alcoholism or drug addiction

Which of the following people in your family have a history of depression or bipolar disorder? Check all that apply.

1. Spouse or partner

2. Mother

3. Father

4. Maternal grandmother

5. Maternal grandfather

6. Paternal grandmother

7. Paternal grandfather

8. Sister

9. Brother

10. Child or children

11. Aunt or uncle

12. No one in my family has a history of depression or bipolar disorder

Mental Illness

1. Do you have a history of any mental health illnesses?
   Yes   No

2. If so, what was/is your diagnosis? _____

3. What kind of treatment have you received for this mental health diagnosis? _____

SUBSTANCE ABUSE

1. Have you ever considered yourself alcoholic or drug-addicted?
   Yes   No

2. If so, for how many years? _____

3. Are you in recovery?

    Yes   No

4. If so, for how many years? _____

5. Did you get into substance abuse recovery before, during, or after recovery from compulsive gambling? _____

GAMBLING HISTORY

1. At what age did you start gambling? _____

2. Types of Gambling:

Please indicate what types of gambling activities you participated in during your gambling. After each type of gambling, answer: "not at all," "less than once a week," or "once a week or more."

	Not at all	Less than once a week	Once a week or more
Poker in card rooms			
Blackjack in card rooms			
Other card games for money			
Pull tabs			
Blackjack in casinos			
Poker in casinos			
Baccarat			
Roulette			
Dice games (including craps)			
Slot machines			
Daily Game/Keno			

Video poker machines			
Lotto/Quinto/Lucky for Life			
Lotteries			
Legal numbers			
Illegal numbers			
Horse racing (OTB, the track, or with a bookie)			
Dog racing (OTB, the track, or with a bookie)			
Bingo			
Sports betting (parlay cards, with a bookie, or at Jai Alai)			
Sports betting (office, job pools)			
Stock, options, and/or commodities market			
Bowl, shoot pool, play golf or play any other game of skill for money			
Other (please identify) _____			

What type of gambling did you start your "gambling career" on, i.e., what type do you think "got you started?" _____

_____

What type(s) of gambling did you feel you were addicted to in the last year before your recovery? _____

_____

Approximately how long did you gamble compulsively before recovery?

1. Six months
2. One year
3. Two years
4. Four years
5. Five years
6. Seven years
7. Ten years
8. Fifteen years
9. Twenty years
10. Over twenty years

What is the largest amount of money you have ever gambled with on any one day?

1. More than $1 but less than $10
2. More than $10 but less than $100
3. More than $100 but less than $1000
4. More than $1000 but less than $5000
5. More than $5000 but less than $10,000
6. More than $10,000

In the last year of your gambling, about how much money do you estimate you were spending per month on gambling?

1. More than $100 but less than $500
2. More than $500 but less than $1000
3. More than $1000 but less than $2000
4. More than $2000 but less than $3000
5. More than $3000 but less than $5000
6. More than $5000 but less than $10,000
7. More than $10,000

What is your estimate of your total financial losses due to gambling?
   1. More than $1000 but less than $5000
   2. More than $5000 but less than $10,000
   3. More than $10,000 but less than $20,000
   4. More than $20,000 but less than $40,000
   5. More than $40,000 but less than $60,000
   6. More than $60,000 but less than $100,000
   7. More than $100,000 but less than $200,000
   8. More than $200,000 but less than $500,000
   9. More than $500,000 but less than $1,000,000
   10. More than $1,000,000

When you quit gambling, what was your total financial debt?
   1. More than $1000 but less than $5000
   2. More than $5000 but less than $10,000
   3. More than $10,000 but less than $20,000
   4. More than $20,000 but less than $40,000
   5. More than $40,000 but less than $60,000
   6. More than $60,000 but less than $100,000
   7. More than $100,000 but less than $200,000
   8. More than $200,000 but less than $500,000
   9. More than $500,000 but less than $1,000,000
   10. More than $1,000,000

When you answered the Gamblers Anonymous Twenty Questions on this Web page, how many questions did you answer Yes? _____

Which of the following describes your gambling behaviors?
Answer "Yes" or "No."

Yes No

☐   ☐   1. Being preoccupied with gambling (e.g., pre-occupied with reliving past gambling experiences, handicapping, or planning the next venture, or thinking of ways to get money with which to gamble).

☐   ☐   2. Needing to gamble with increasing amounts of money to achieve desired excitement.

☐   ☐   3. Having repeated unsuccessful efforts to cut back or stop gambling.

☐   ☐   4. Being restless or irritable when attempting to cut down or stop.

☐   ☐   5. Gambling as a way of escaping problems or of relieving dysphoric mood (e.g., feelings of helplessness, guilt, anxiety, depression).

☐   ☐   6. After losing money gambling, often returning another day to get even ("chasing" one's losses).

☐   ☐   7. Lying to family members, therapist, or others to conceal extent of involvement with gambling.

☐   ☐   8. Committing illegal acts such as forgery, fraud, theft, or embezzlement to finance gambling.

☐   ☐   9. Jeopardizing or losing a significant relationship, job, or educational or career opportunity because of gambling.

☐   ☐   10. Relying on others to provide money to relieve a desperate financial situation caused by gambling.

Which of the following reasons influenced you to start serious gambling? Answer "Yes" or "No."

Yes No

☐ ☐ 1. Escaping from worries or troubles with spouse/partner

☐ ☐ 2. Escaping from worries or troubles on the job

☐ ☐ 3. Feeling lonely

☐ ☐ 4. Looking for action or excitement

☐ ☐ 5. Bored with routine of my life

☐ ☐ 6. Getting even with someone

☐ ☐ 7. Wanting to cover debt or losses

☐ ☐ 8. Spouse/partner died

☐ ☐ 9. Divorced/separated from my spouse/partner

☐ ☐ 10. Children left home

☐ ☐ 11. Retired from work

☐ ☐ 12. Feeling depressed about my life and future

☐ ☐ 13. Had a big win and wanted to repeat it

☐ ☐ 14. Mother died

☐ ☐ 15. Father died

☐ ☐ 16. Looking for fun and recreation

☐ ☐ 17. Hoping to get rich

☐ ☐ Other? _____

The following is a list of common results from compulsive gambling and from trying to cover your losses. Which of these effects did you experience? Answer "Yes" or "No."

Yes No

☐ ☐ Physical health seriously deteriorated

☐ ☐ Children removed from home by child welfare

☐ ☐ Spouse or partner left you

☐ ☐ Divorce

☐ ☐ Declared bankruptcy

☐ ☐ Borrowed money from friends

☐ ☐ Borrowed money from family

☐ ☐ Unable to pay back money from friends/family

☐ ☐ Took money from retirement savings to gamble

☐ ☐ Cashed in all my retirement, IRAs, savings

☐ ☐ Attempted suicide

☐ ☐ Left children unsupervised while gambling

☐ ☐ Lost job because of gambling

☐ ☐ Wrote bad checks

☐ ☐ Embezzled/stole money from work

☐ ☐ Had payroll check garnished

☐ ☐ Spent time in jail/prison for crimes related to gambling

☐ ☐ Lost a business

☐ ☐ Lost my house because I couldn't make the payments

☐ ☐ Lost a relationship with children

☐ ☐ Lost a relationship with friends

☐ ☐ Lost a relationship with parents

☐ ☐ Victim of physical violence from spouse/partner as a result of gambling

☐ ☐ Victim of verbal/emotional abuse from spouse/partner as a result of gambling

☐ ☐ Physically violent with children because of gambling

☐ ☐ Verbally abusive toward children because of gambling

☐ ☐ Physically violent with spouse because of gambling

☐ ☐ Verbally abusive toward spouse because of gambling

☐ ☐ Forged checks

☐ ☐ Engaged in prostitution

☐ ☐ Engaged in bookmaking or working in an illegal game

☐ ☐ Engaged in loan fraud

☐ ☐ Engaged in other illegal activities for money

☐ ☐ Hospitalized for a mental illness

☐ ☐ Gambled whole paycheck

☐ ☐ Gambled whole welfare, SSI, or Social Security check

☐ ☐ Evicted from my house or apartment

☐ ☐ Homeless

☐ ☐ Stopped attending church or maintaining any spiritual practices

☐ ☐ Lied to family about losses

☐ ☐ Lied to family about my whereabouts when gambling

Other effects (please explain) _____

_____

When you look back over your compulsive gambling days, what do you regret the very most? _____

_____

RECOVERY HISTORY

How long have you been abstinent from gambling?
Number of years: _____ Months: _____

More than anything, what made you stop gambling? _____

_____

_____

Did you quit gambling "on your own" without benefit of GA or professional help?

    Yes   No

If yes, please describe how you did it: _____

_____

_____

Did you receive professional help to assist you in quitting gambling?

    Yes   No

If yes, please describe: _____

_____

_____

_____

What was the frequency of this professional help?

    1. One session every few months

    2. One session a month

    3. One session a week

    4. Two sessions a week

    5. More than two sessions a week

    6. Did not receive professional help

Did you ever participate in day treatment for gambling?

    Yes   No

Did you ever participate in inpatient treatment for gambling?

    Yes   No

Approximately what was the duration of your professional help?

    1. 1–3 months

    2. 3–6 months

    3. 6–9 months

4. 9–12 months

5. More than 1 year but less than 2 years

6. Over 2 years

7. Did not receive professional help

Did your counselor/therapist refer you to Gamblers Anonymous?

Yes   No

Did you ever seek professional help and then not mention your compulsive gambling?

Yes   No

If yes, describe reasons: _____

_____

_____

Have you ever been to a social service agency (crisis center, employee assistance, family service agency, mental health agency, etc.) to discuss your gambling?

Yes   No

If yes, please explain: _____

_____

_____

Did you attend Gamblers Anonymous meetings prior to quitting gambling?

Yes   No

Approximately how often did you attend GA meetings before you actually quit gambling?

1. Two or more times a week

2. Once a week

3. Once a month

4. Once every few months

5. Once a year
6. Once every few years
7. Never attended

How long did you attend meetings before quitting gambling?
Estimate from the time you attended your first GA meeting:
1. 1–3 months
2. 3–6 months
3. 6–9 months
4. 9–12 months
5. More than 1 year but less than 2 years
6. More than 2 years but less than 3 years
7. More than 3 years but less than 5 years
8. More than 5 years but less than 10 years
9. More than 10 years
10. Never attended

Who referred you to GA?
1. I called the 1-800-Help Line in my state
2. A friend who was in GA
3. A family member who was in GA
4. A professional counselor
5. Yellow pages in the phone book
6. Substance abuse treatment center
7. Never referred to GA
8. Other _____

If you attended GA, in what ways, if any, did you feel welcomed?
_____
_____

In what, if any, ways did you feel unwelcome at GA? _____
_____
_____

Do you attend GA now?

Yes   No

How often in the last year?

1. Two or more times a week
2. Once a week
3. Once a month
4. Once every few months
5. Once a year
6. Once every few years
7. Do not attend

How often did you attend GA in your first year of recovery?

1. Two or more times a week
2. Once a week
3. Once a month
4. Once every few months
5. Once a year
6. Once every few years
7. Do not attend

Do you sponsor anyone in GA?

Yes   No

How many persons have you sponsored since your recovery? _____

What could GA do to attract more women? _____

_____

_____

_____

Of the following support systems, which was the most important to help you stop gambling?

1. Psychologist
2. Social worker
3. Gamblers Anonymous
4. Spouse or partner
5. Children
6. Parents
7. Work-related support
8. Church/Religious group
9. Minister/priest
10. Probation/parole officer
11. Family physician
12. Other self-help group (AA, NA)
13. Treatment program for compulsive gambling
14. Treatment program for substance abuse
15. Other source of support: _____

Did your spouse or partner or relative/friend attend Gam-Anon?
Yes   No

Does your spouse or partner or relative/friend continue to attend Gam-Anon?
Yes   No

If so, how often in the last year?

1. Two or more times a week
2. Once a week
3. Once a month
4. Once every few months
5. Once a year
6. Once every few years
7. Did not attend Gam-Anon

Which answer best describes your experience of your spouse/
partner attending Gam-Anon?

    1. Very helpful to me and my recovery

    2. Somewhat helpful to me and my recovery

    3. Somewhat unhelpful to me and my recovery

    4. Unhelpful to me and my recovery

    5. Did not attend Gam-Anon

When you look over your time in recovery from compulsive gambling, what makes you the most proud? _____

_____

_____

_____

What advice would you give social workers, psychologists, and
other professional counselors about helping women get into recovery from compulsive gambling? _____

_____

_____

_____

About the Author

Diane Rae Davis is a professor of social work at Eastern Washington University, with a Ph.D. from the University of Texas at Austin. She is the coauthor of *Addiction Treatment: A Strengths Perspective* with Katherine van Wormer, and has written articles from her research on problem gambling, Alcoholics Anonymous, alcohol and drug treatment, and harm reduction. Before her academic life, she was a practicing social worker in Austin, Texas, in the mental health field.

Hazelden, a national nonprofit organization founded in 1949, helps people reclaim their lives from the disease of addiction. Built on decades of knowledge and experience, Hazelden offers a comprehensive approach to addiction that addresses the full range of patient, family, and professional needs, including treatment and continuing care for youth and adults, research, higher learning, public education and advocacy, and publishing. A life of recovery is lived "one day at a time." Hazelden publications, both educational and inspirational, support and strengthen lifelong recovery. In 1954, Hazelden published *Twenty-Four Hours a Day,* the first daily meditation book for recovering alcoholics, and Hazelden continues to publish works to inspire and guide individuals in treatment and recovery, and their loved ones. Professionals who work to prevent and treat addiction also turn to Hazelden for evidence-based curricula, informational materials, and videos for use in schools, treatment programs, and correctional programs. Through published works, Hazelden extends the reach of hope, encouragement, help, and support to individuals, families, and communities affected by addiction and related issues.

For questions about Hazelden publications,
please call 800-328-9000
or visit us online at hazelden.org/bookstore.